# SEPTEMBER 50 COLORING PAGES FOR OLDER KIDS RELAXATION

## SHIH CHIEN HUA

I0481736

PUBLISHED BY:
SHIH CHIEN HUA
Copyright © 2018

SEABIRD SHOP >50FOR

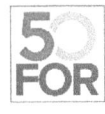

FB  FAN PAGE

**Disclaimer**
The information contained in this book is for general information purposes only. The information is provided by the authors and while we endeavor to keep the information up to date and correct, we make no representations or warranties of any kind, express or implied, about the completeness, accuracy, reliability, suitability or availability with respect to the book or the information, products, services, or related graphics contained in the book for any purpose. Any reliance you place on such information is therefore strictly at your own risk.

# SEPTEMBER 1ST

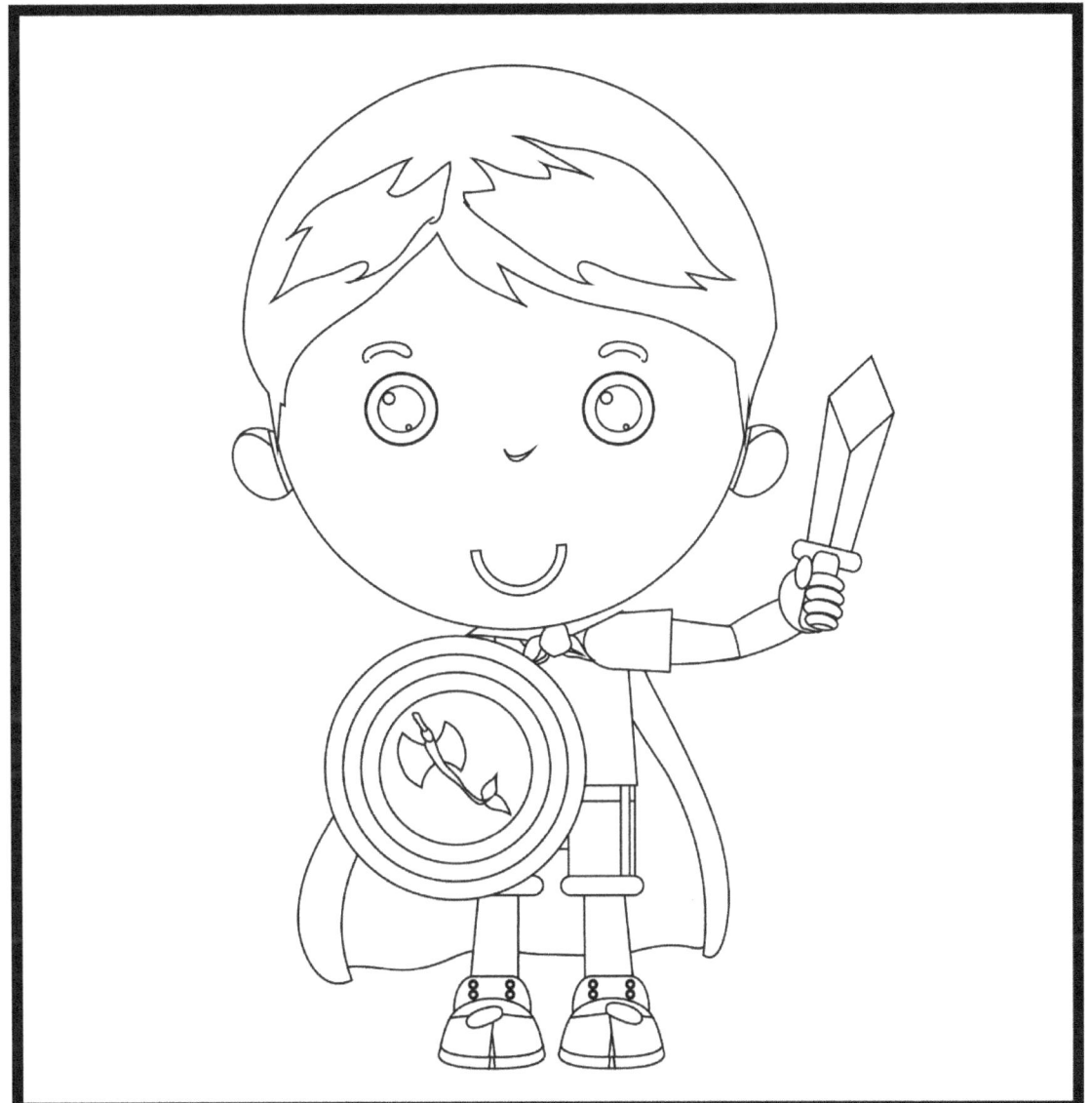

note:

_____

_____

_____

# SEPTEMBER 2ND

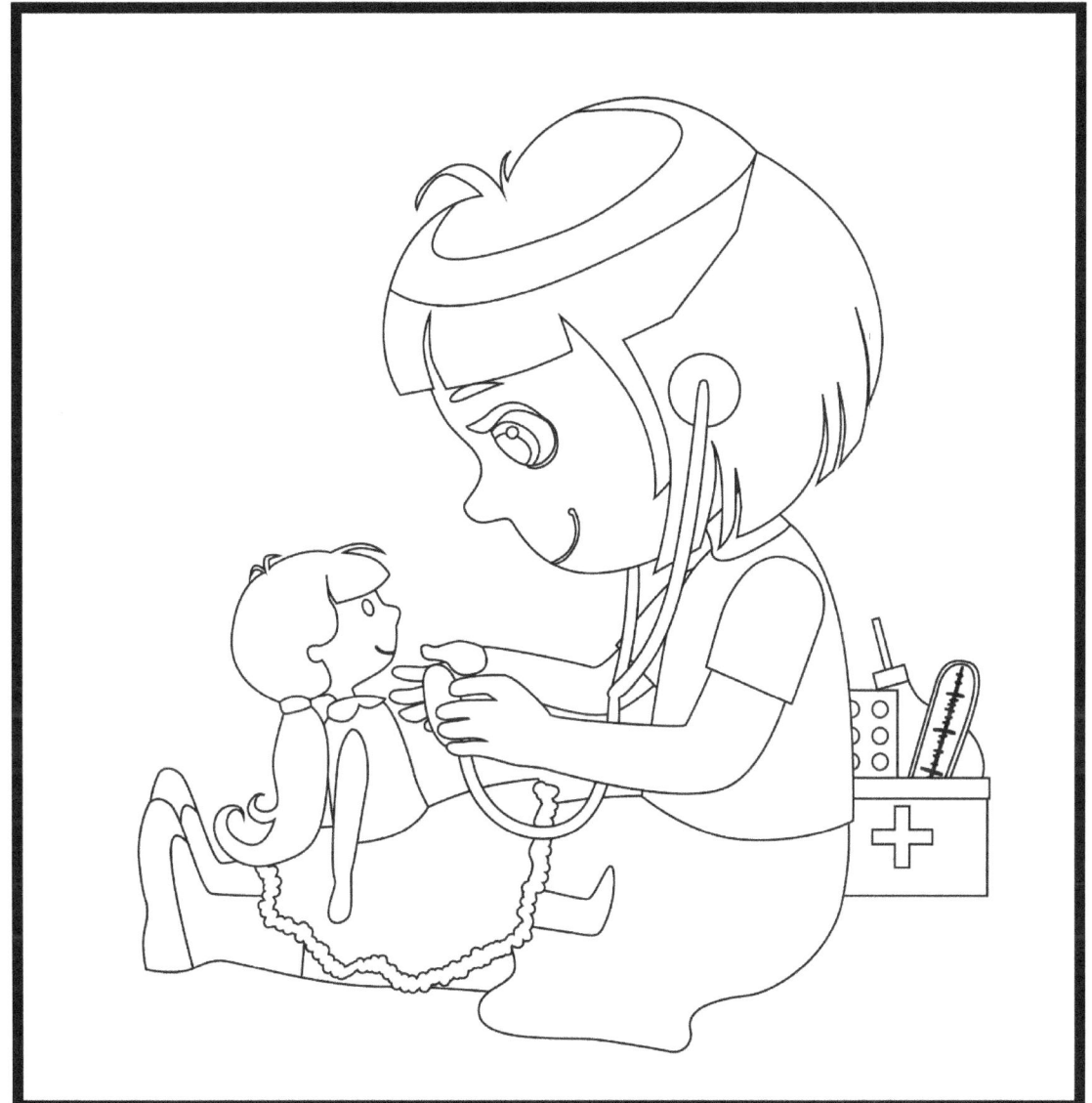

note:

_____

_____

_____

# SEPTEMBER 3RD

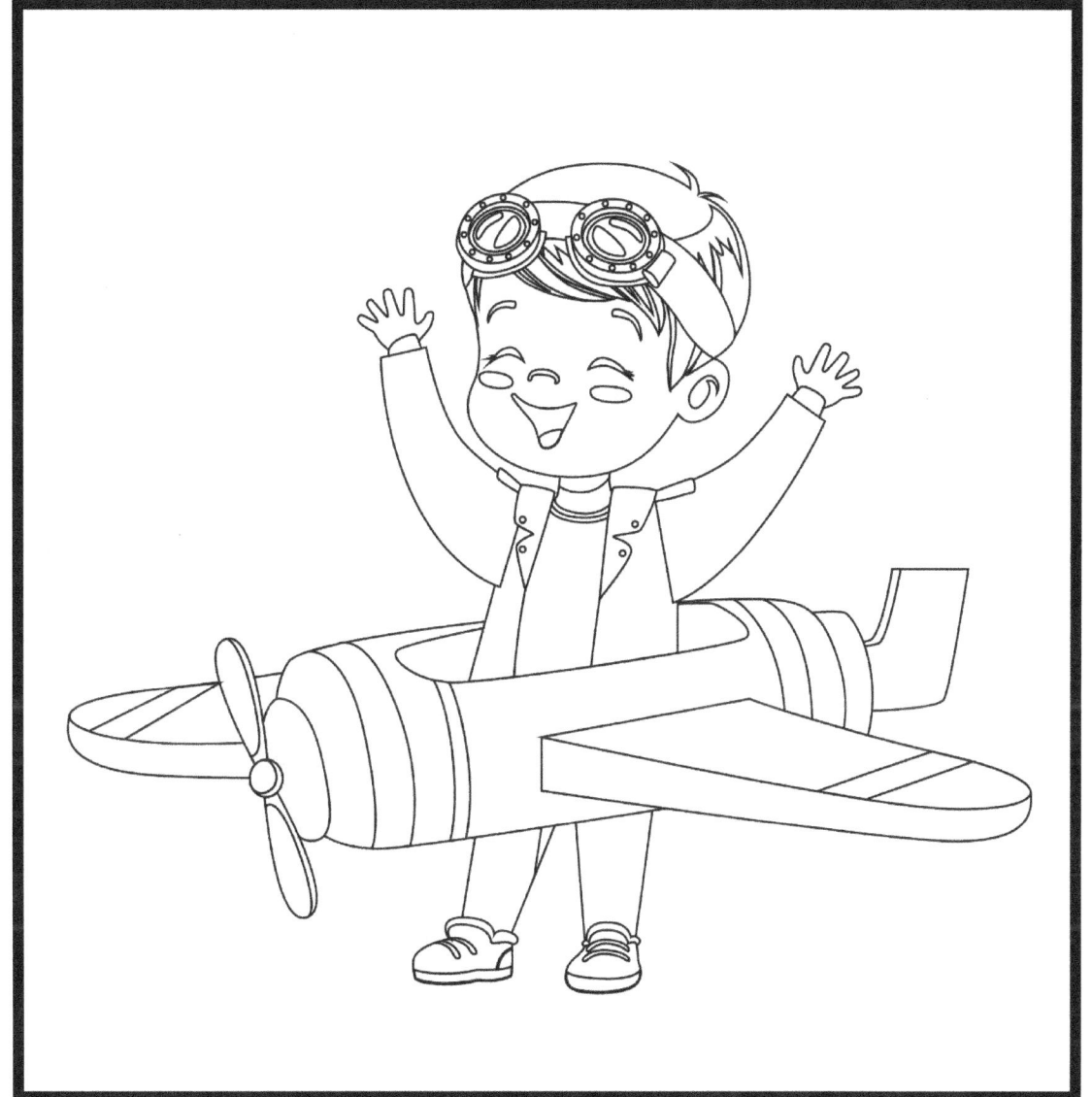

note:

_____

_____

_____

# SEPTEMBER 4TH

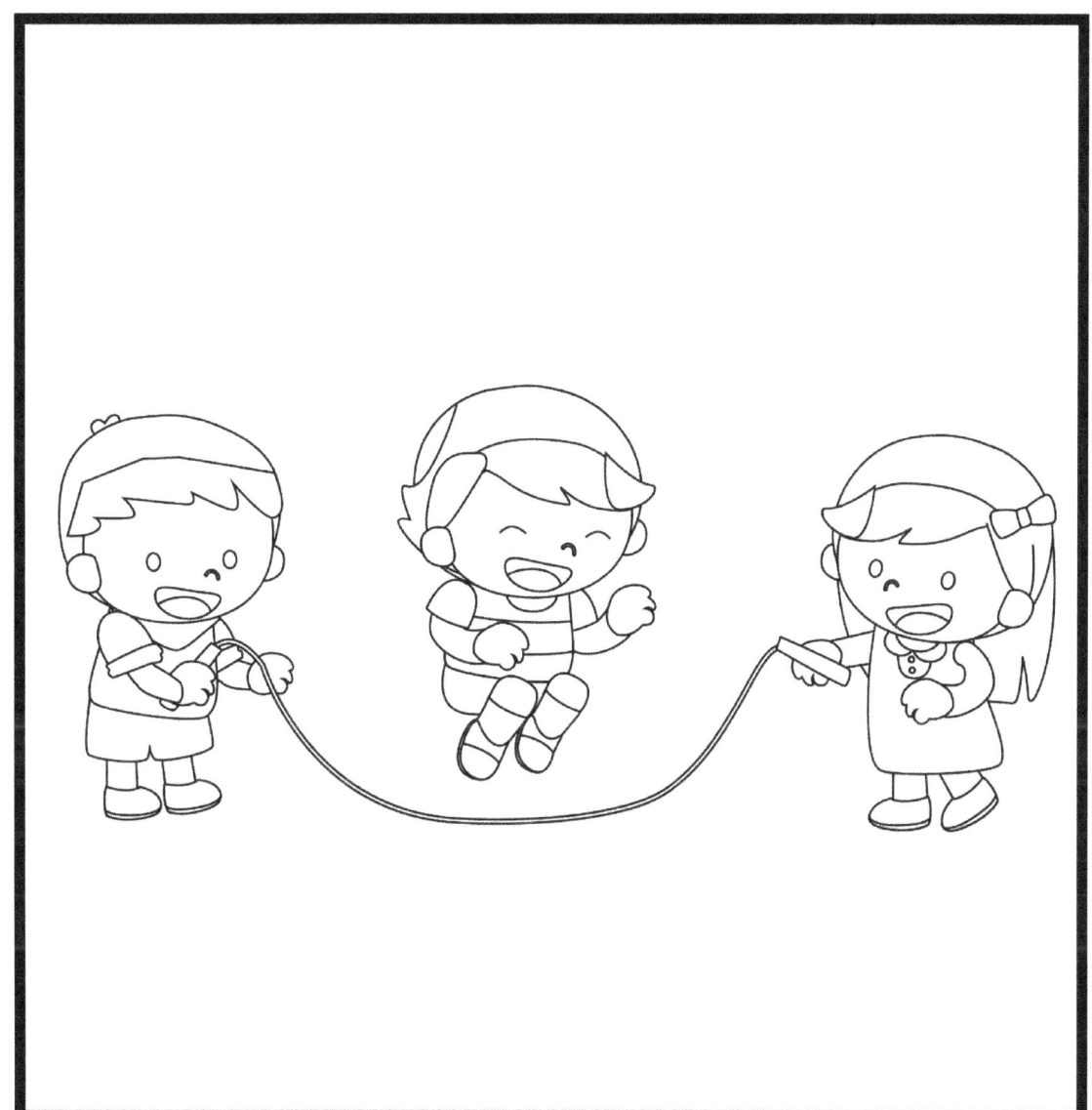

note:

_____

_____

_____

# SEPTEMBER 5TH

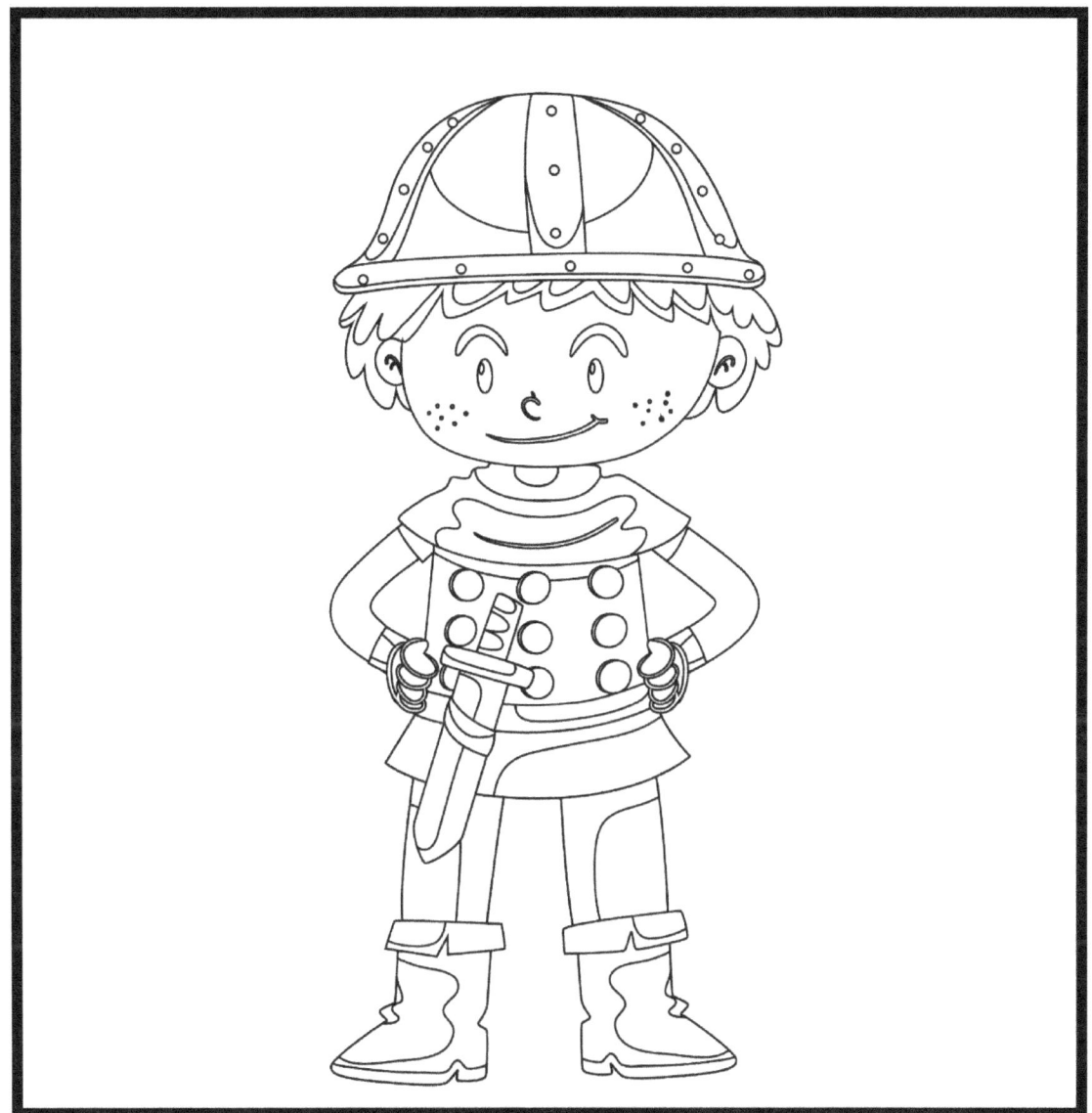

note:

_____

_____

_____

# SEPTEMBER 6TH

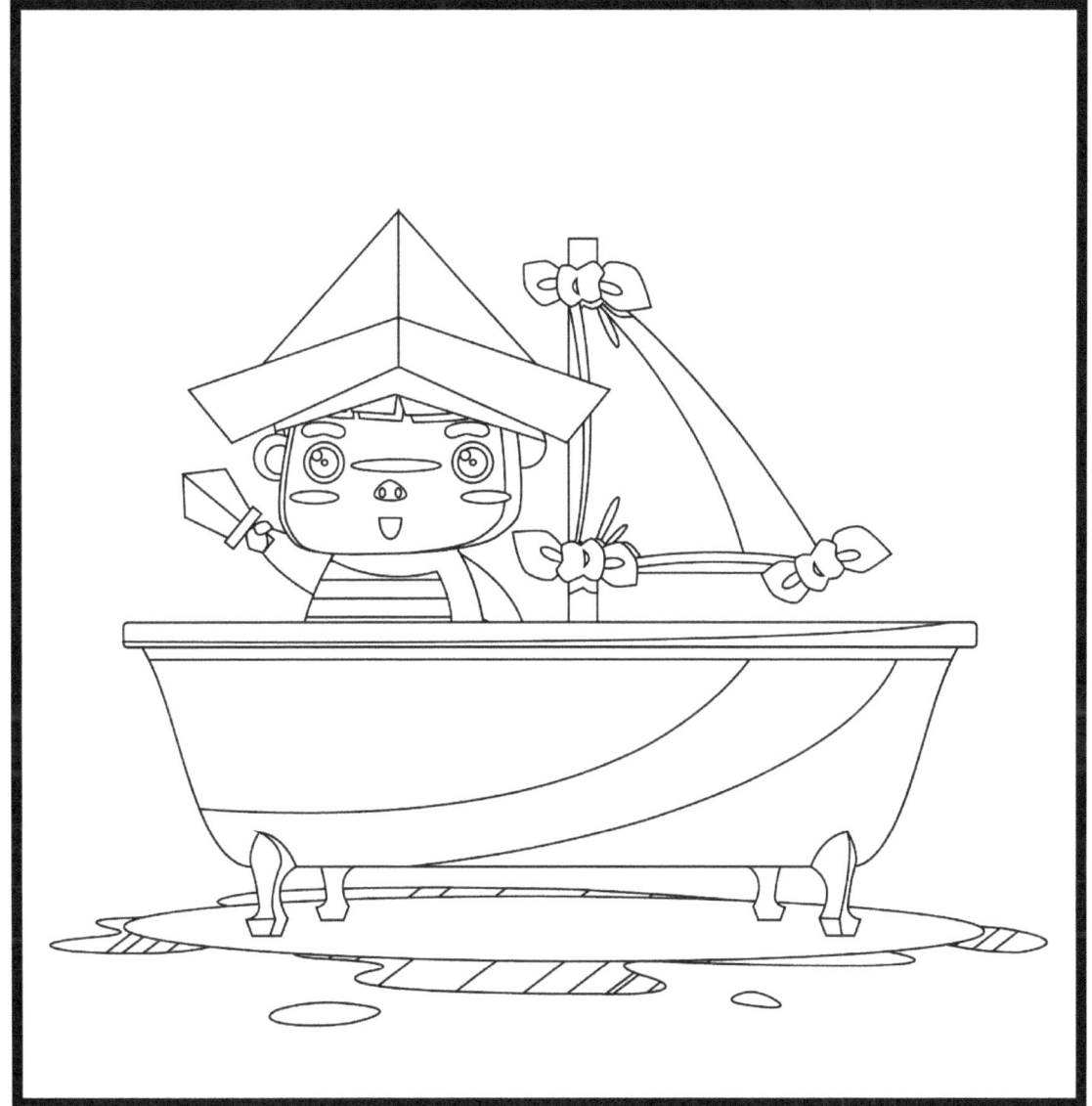

note:

_____

_____

_____

# SEPTEMBER 7TH

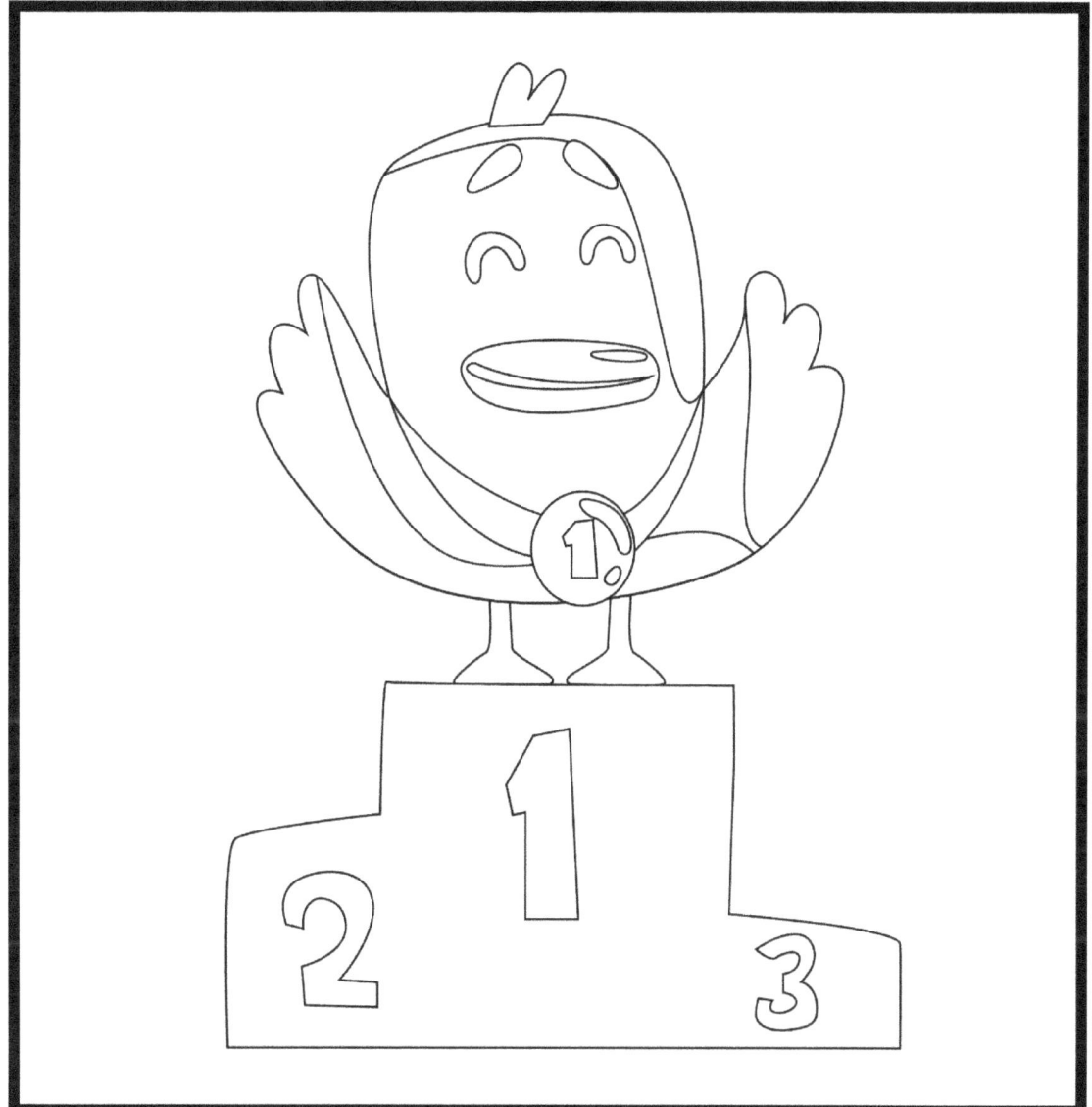

note:

_____

_____

_____

# SEPTEMBER 8TH

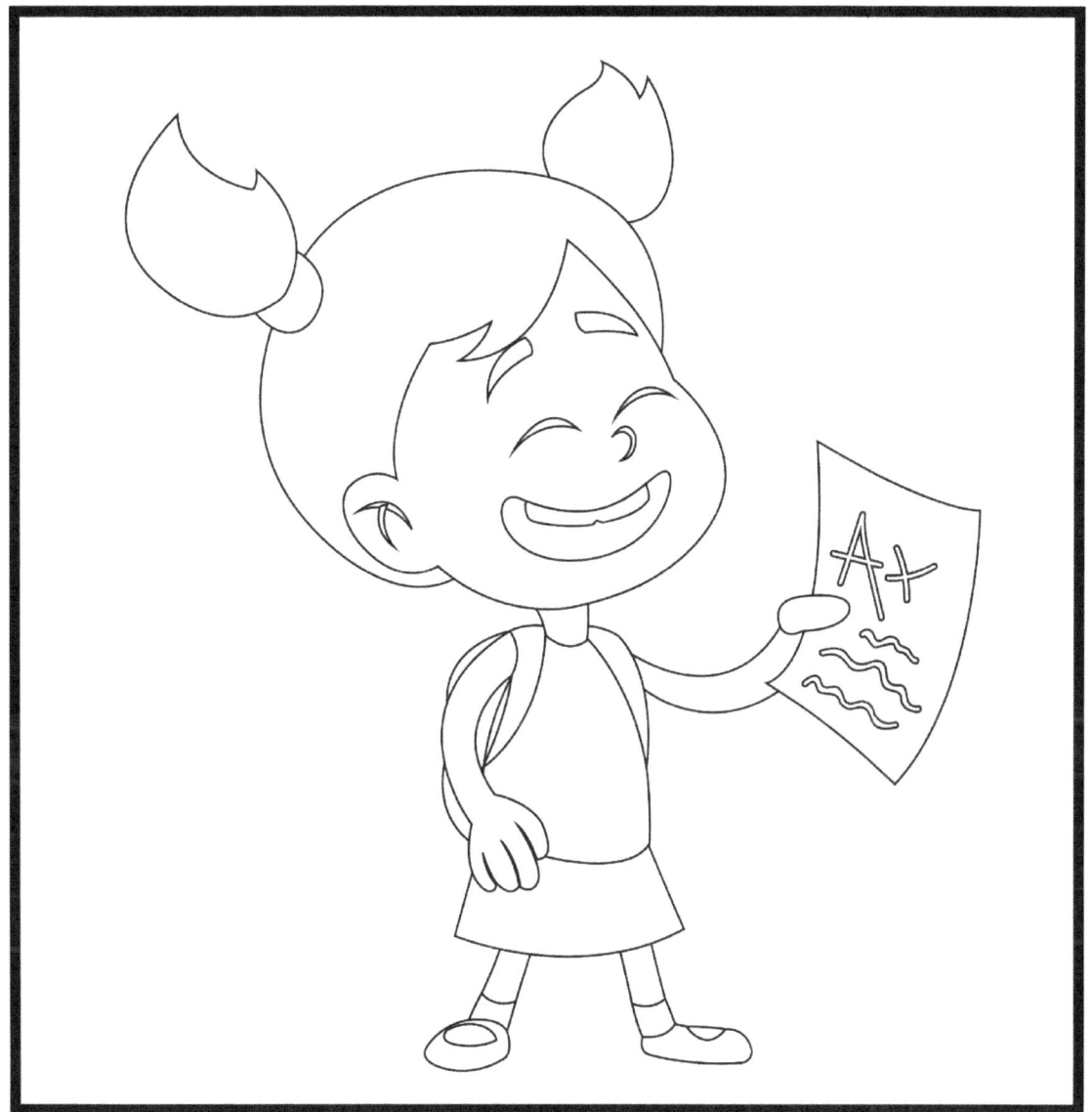

note:

_____

_____

_____

# SEPTEMBER 9TH

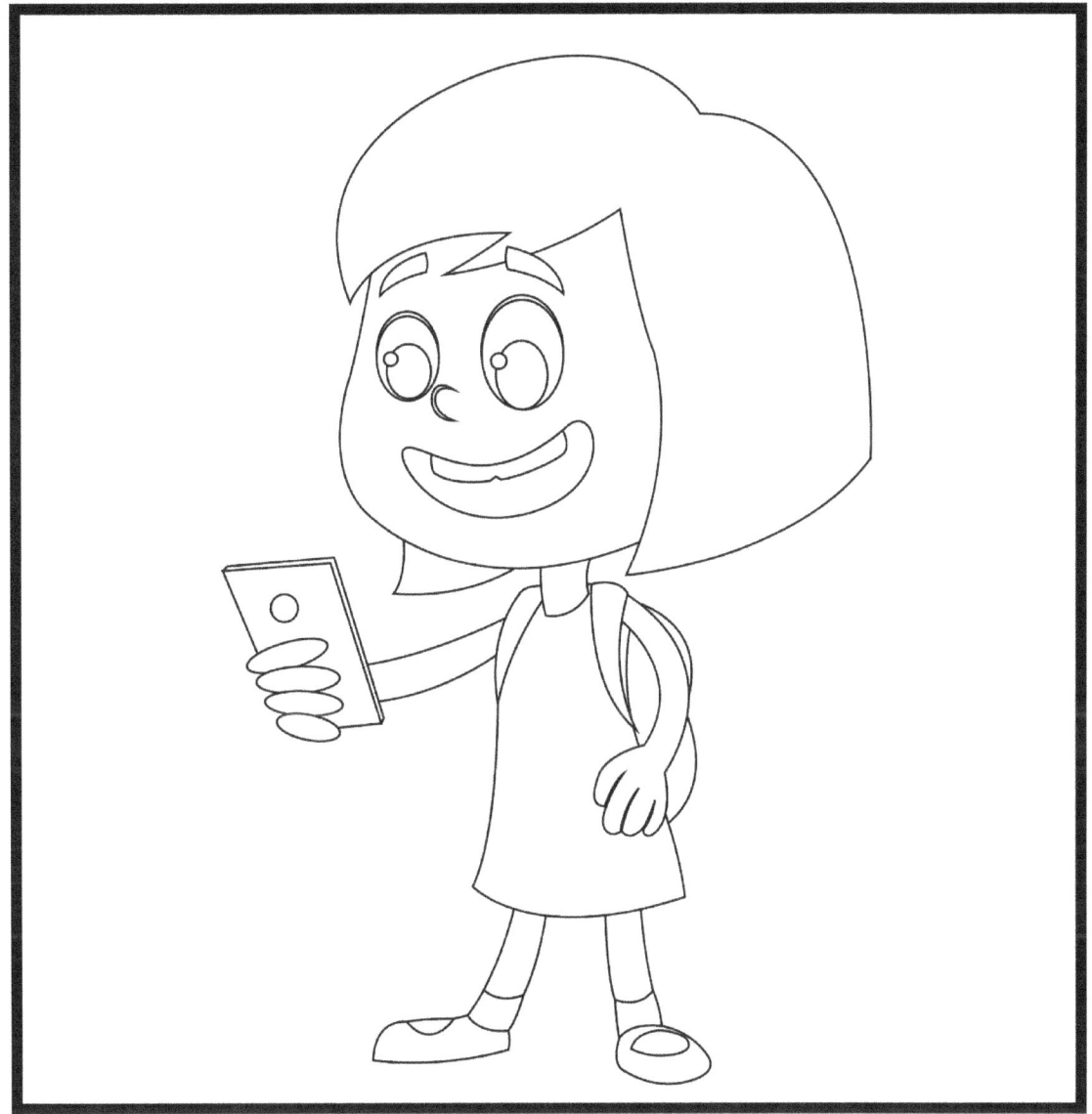

note:

_____

_____

_____

# SEPTEMBER 10TH

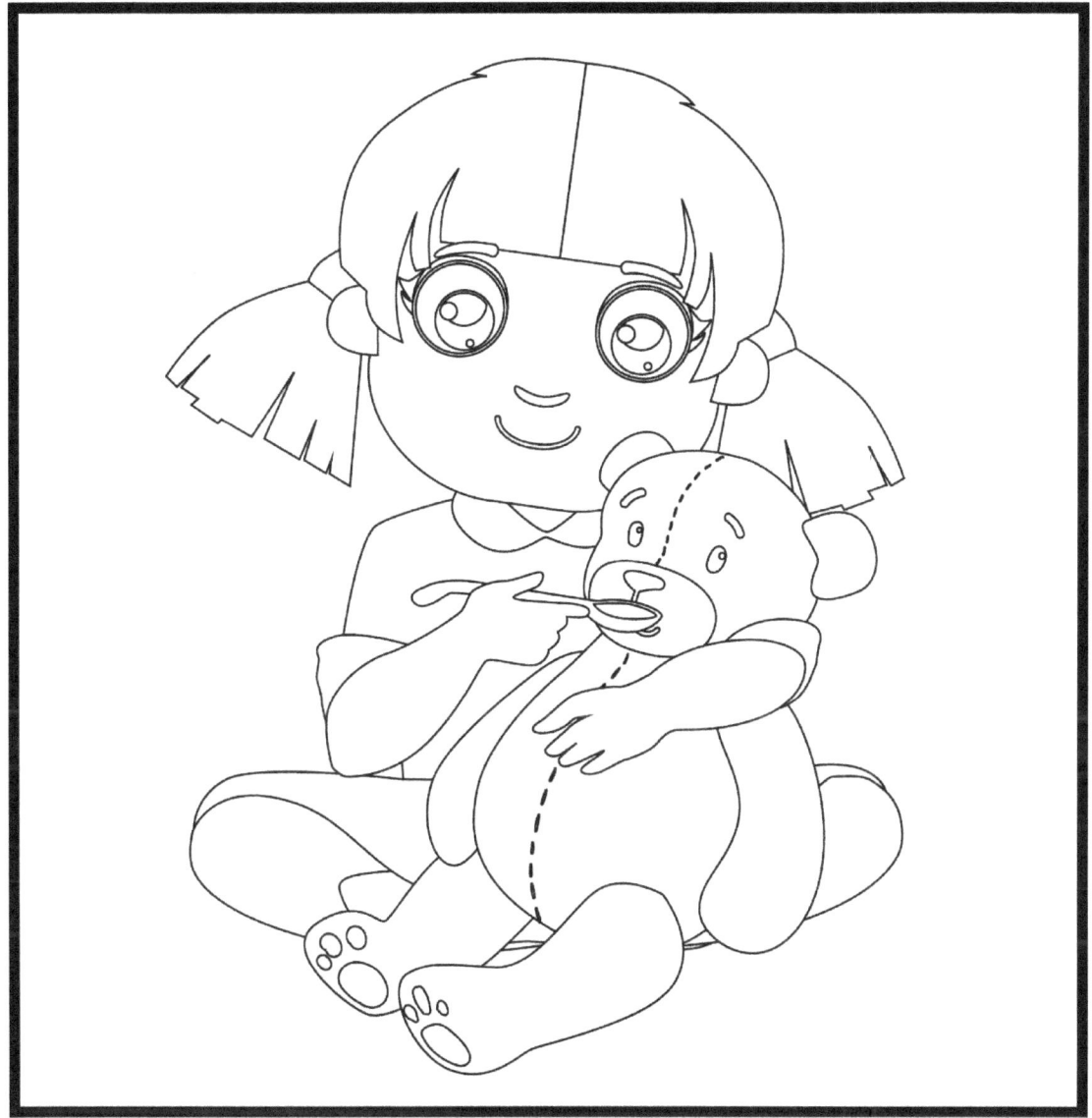

note:

_____

_____

_____

# SEPTEMBER 11TH

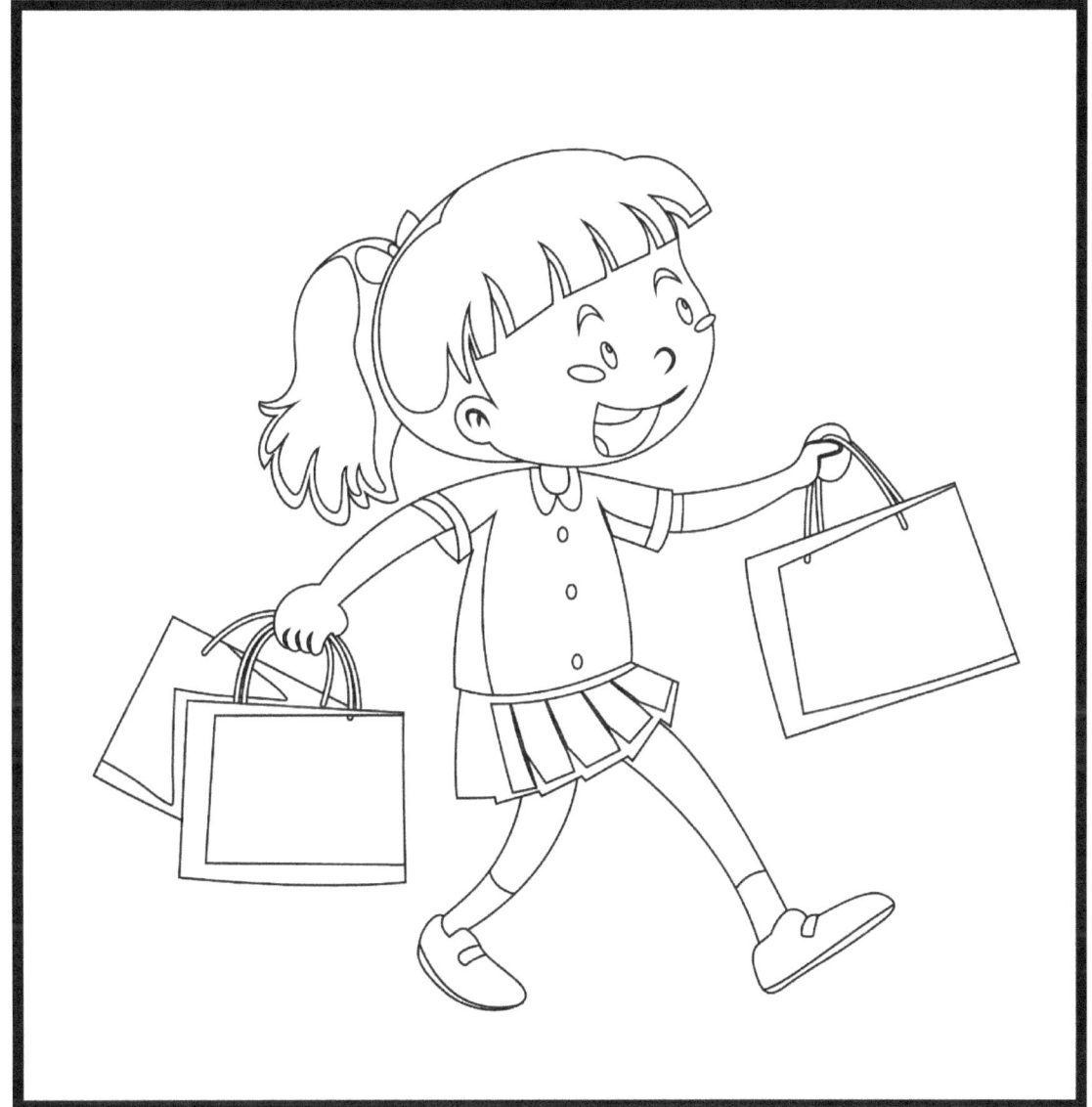

note:

_____

_____

_____

# SEPTEMBER 12TH

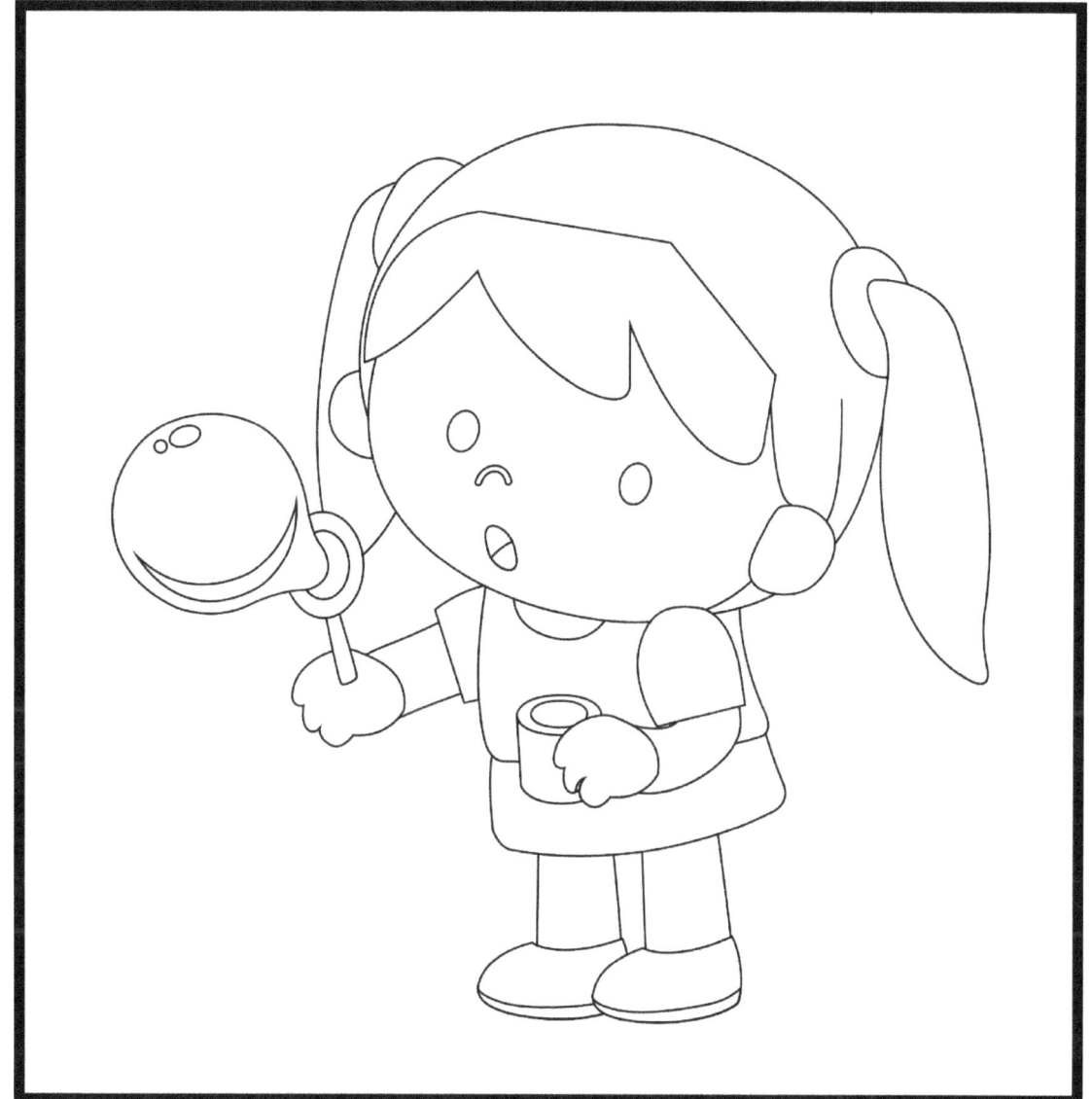

note:

_____

_____

_____

# SEPTEMBER 13TH

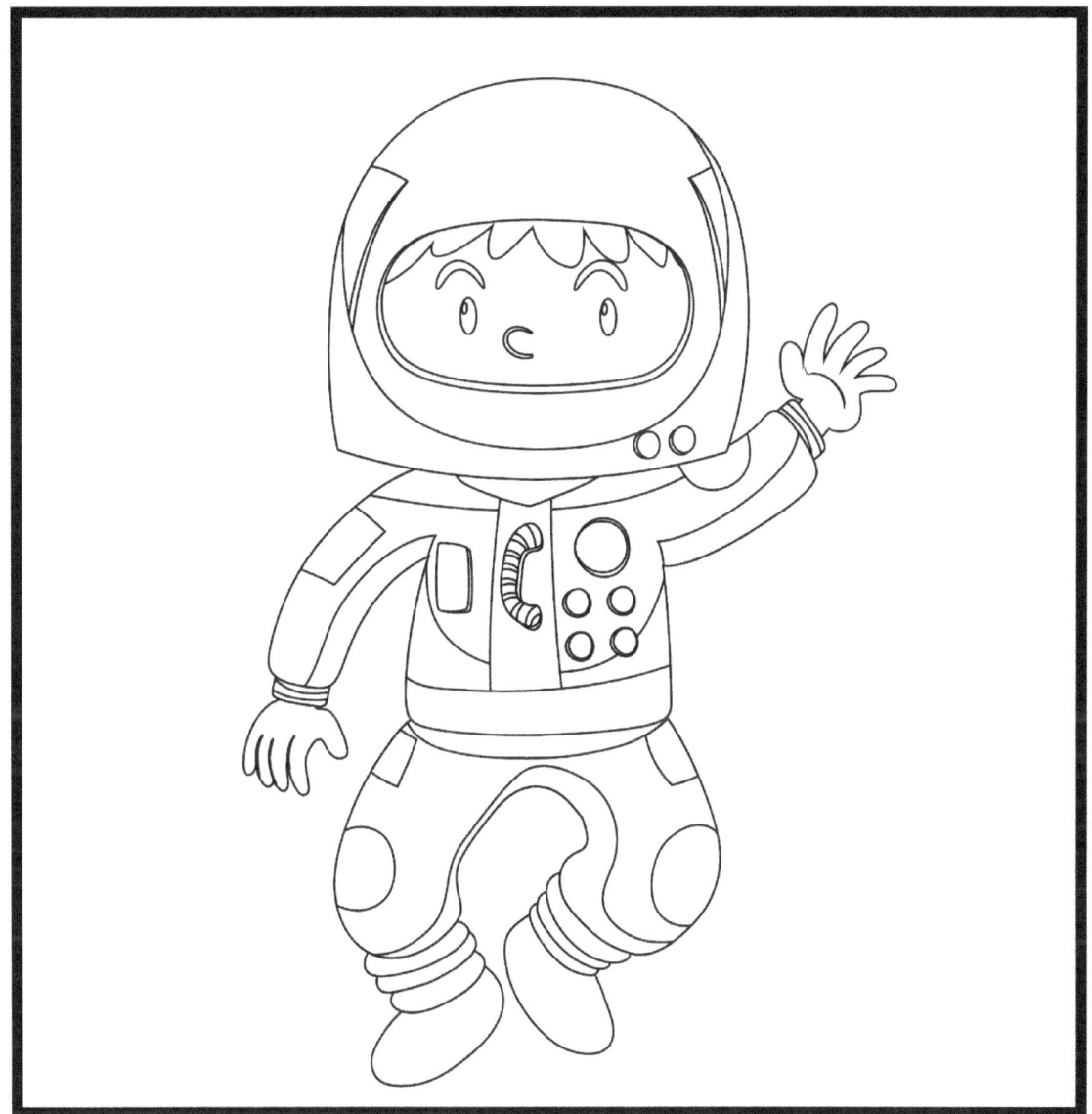

note:

_____

_____

_____

# SEPTEMBER 14TH

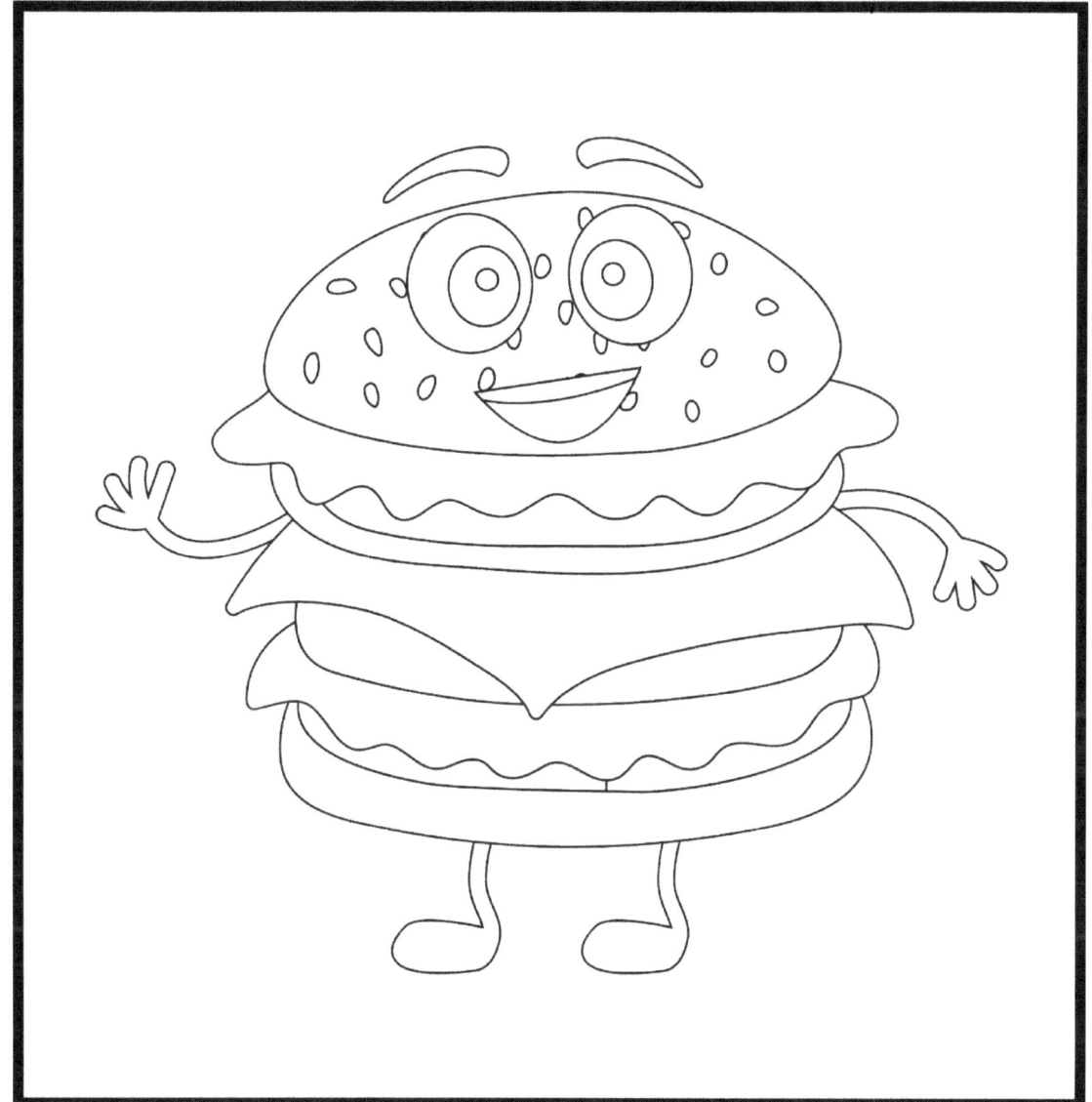

note:

_____

_____

_____

# SEPTEMBER 15TH

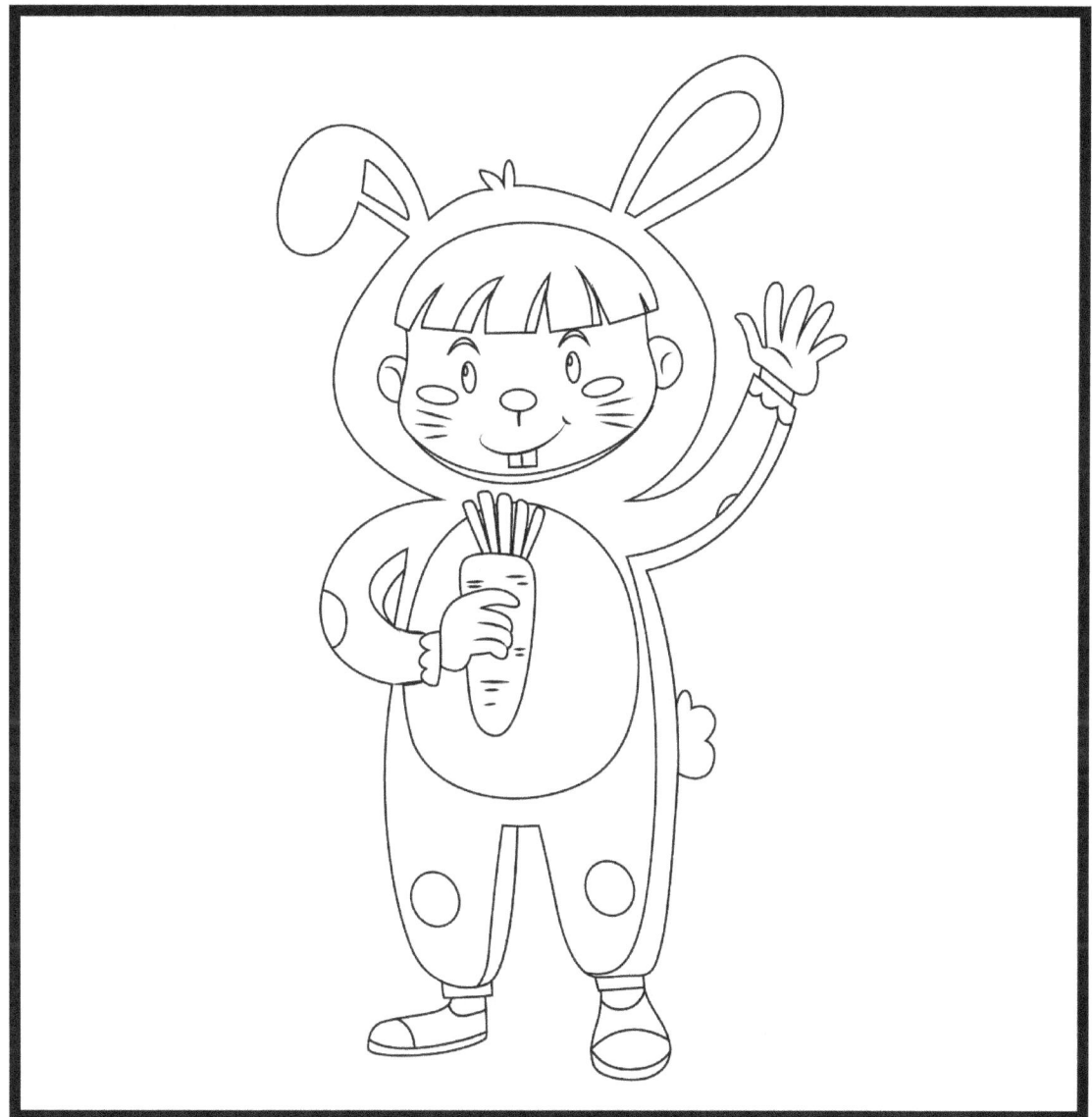

note:

_____

_____

_____

# SEPTEMBER 16TH

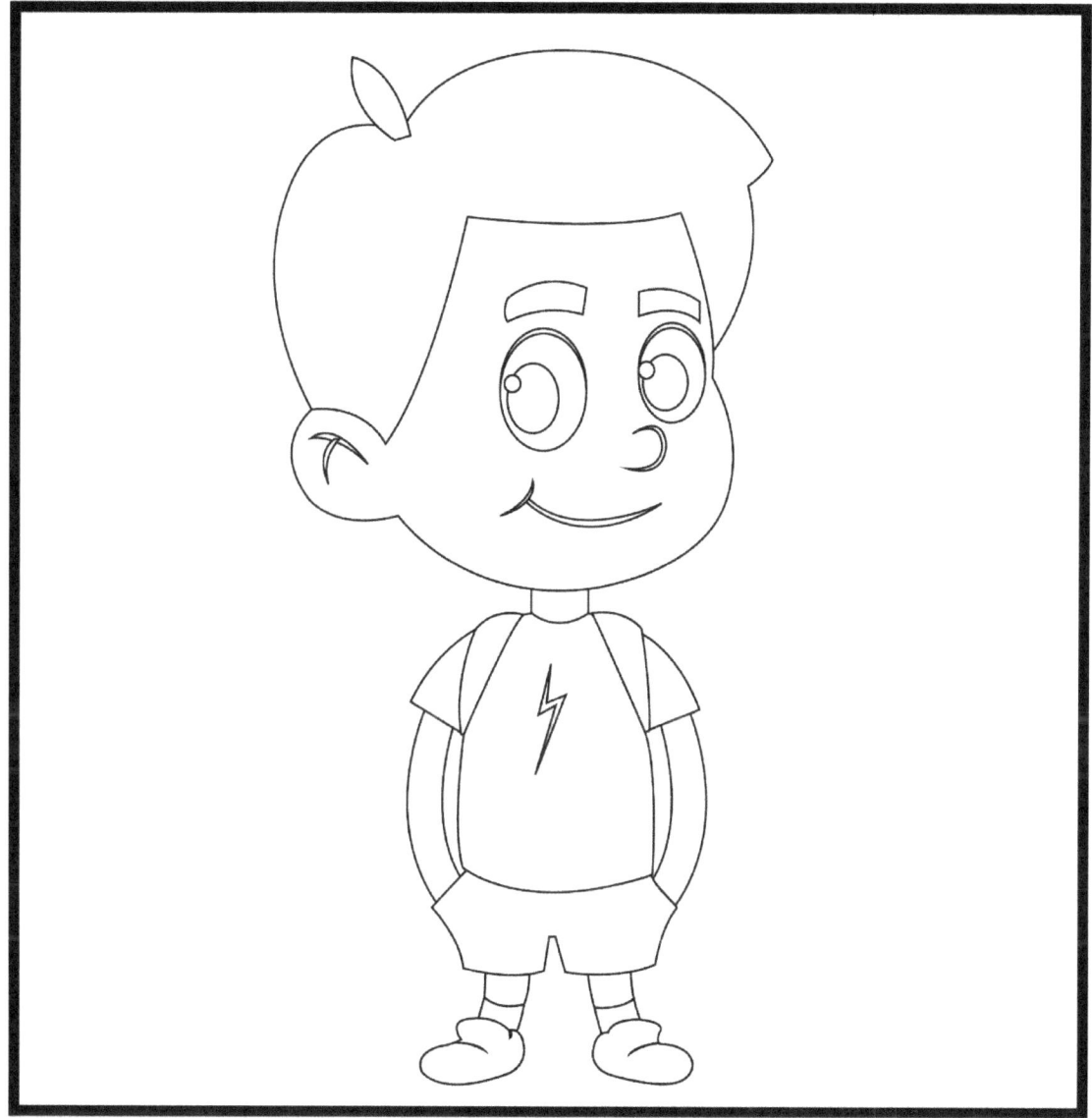

note:

_____

_____

_____

# SEPTEMBER 17TH

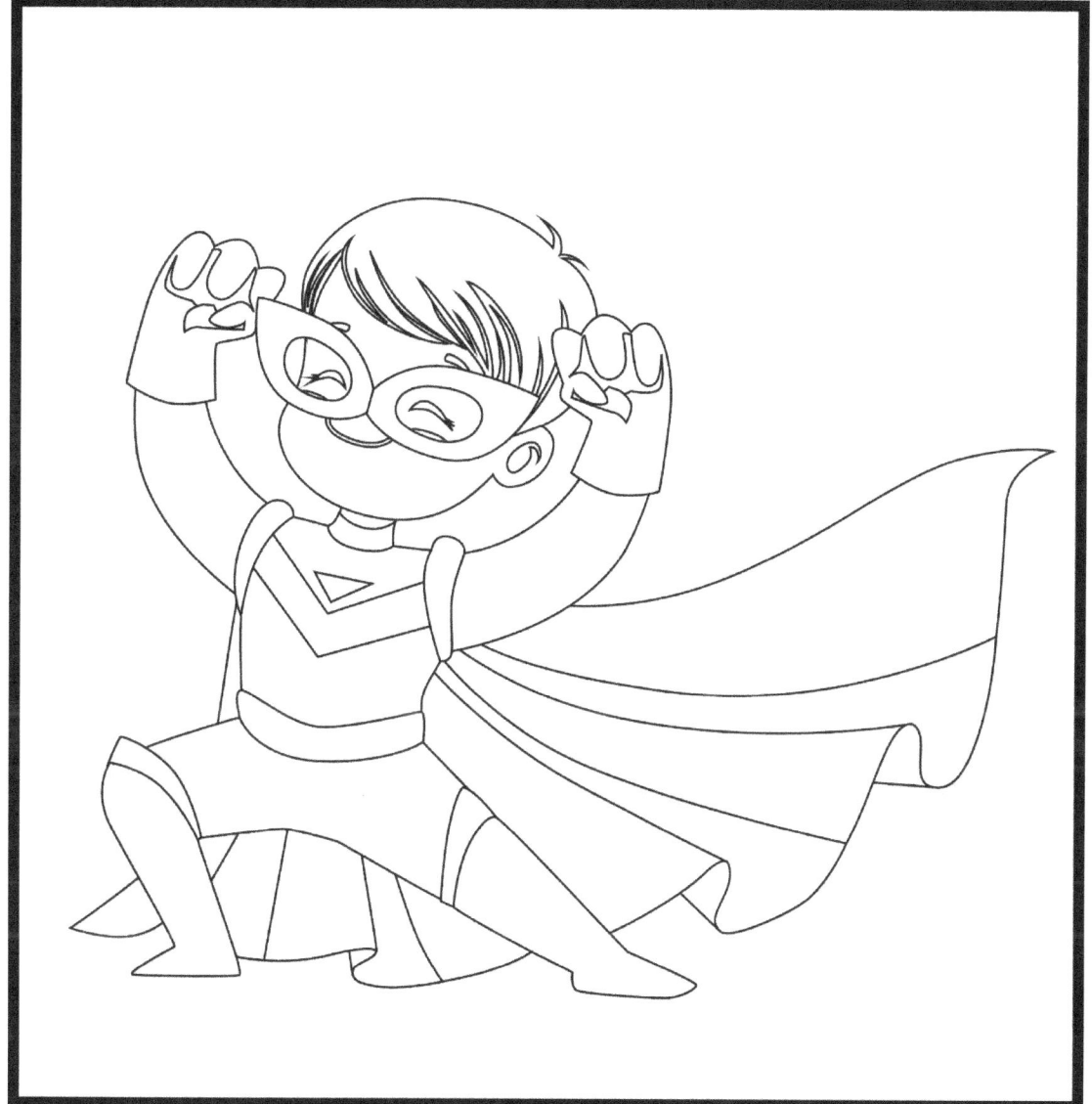

note:

_____

_____

_____

# SEPTEMBER 18TH

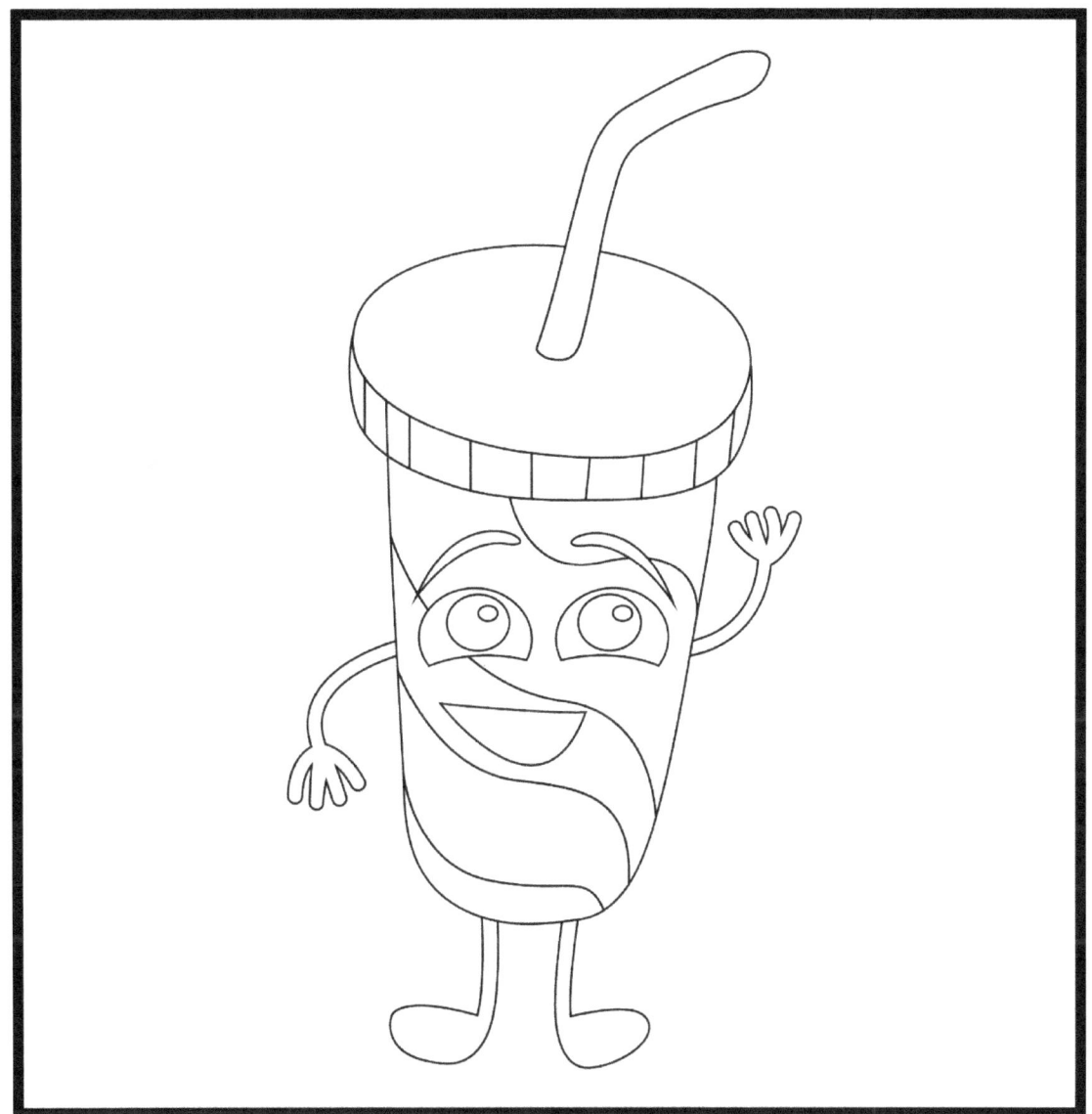

note:

_____

_____

_____

# SEPTEMBER 19TH

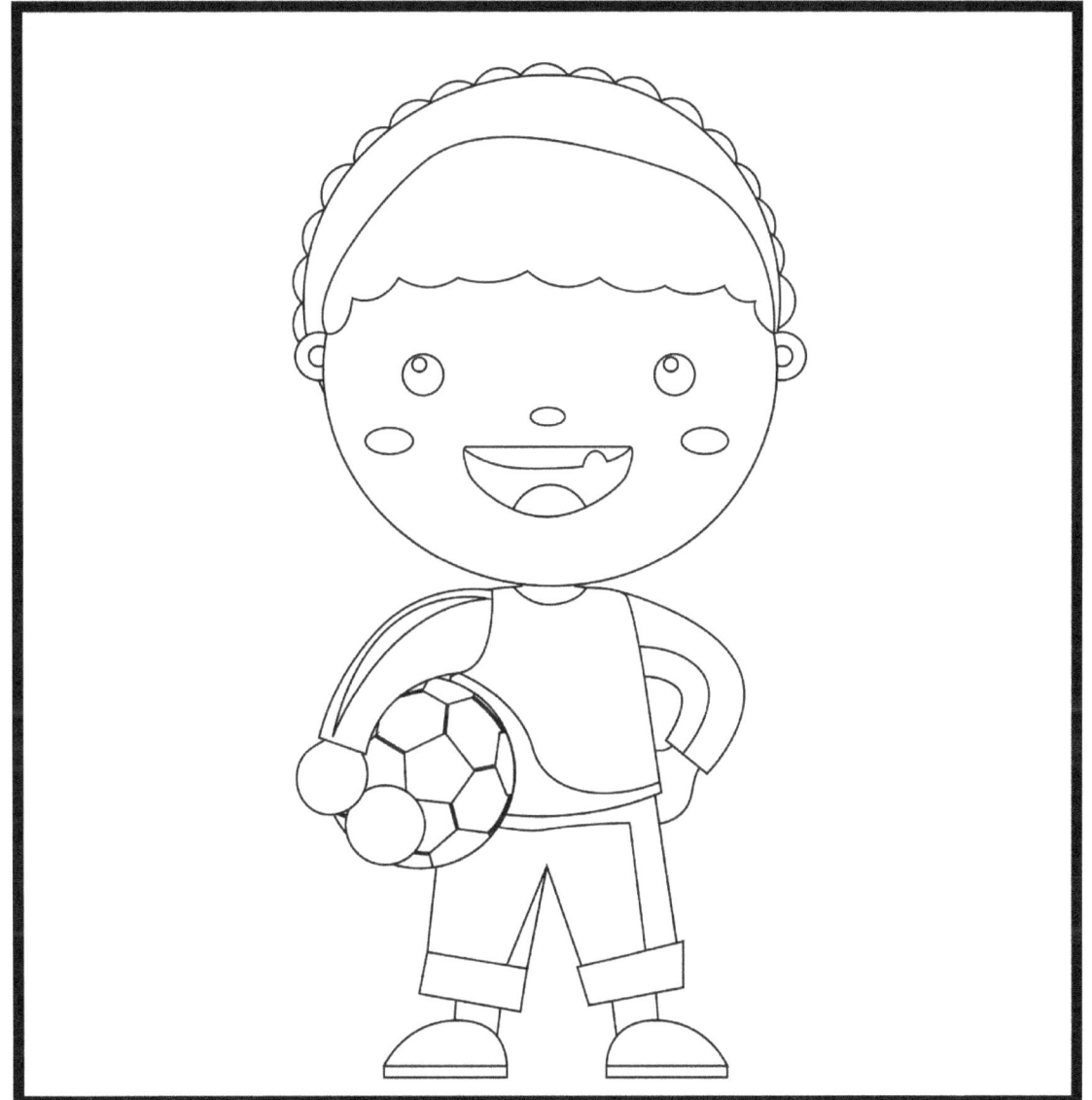

note:

_____

_____

_____

# SEPTEMBER 20TH

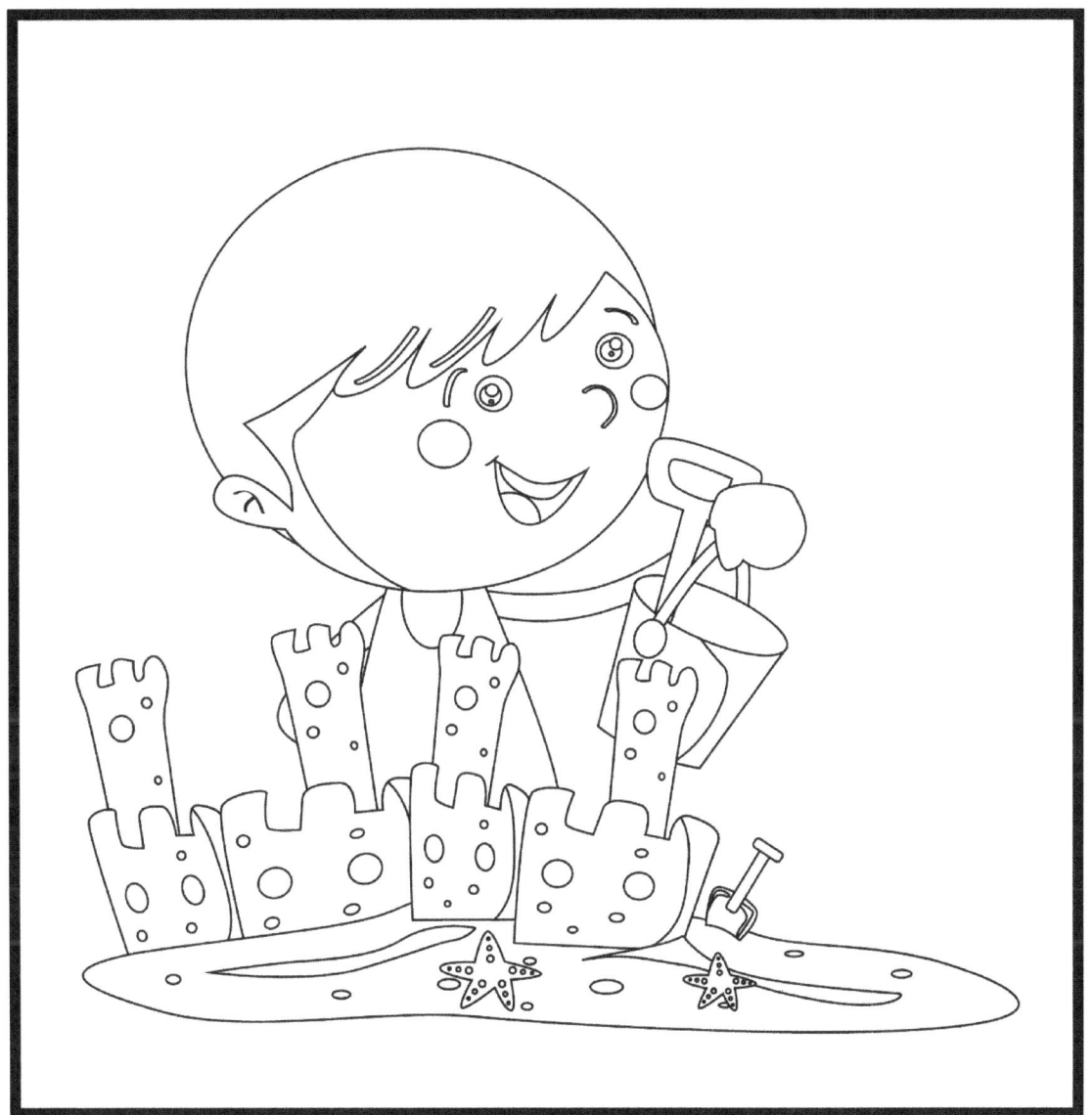

note:

_____

_____

_____

# SEPTEMBER 21TH

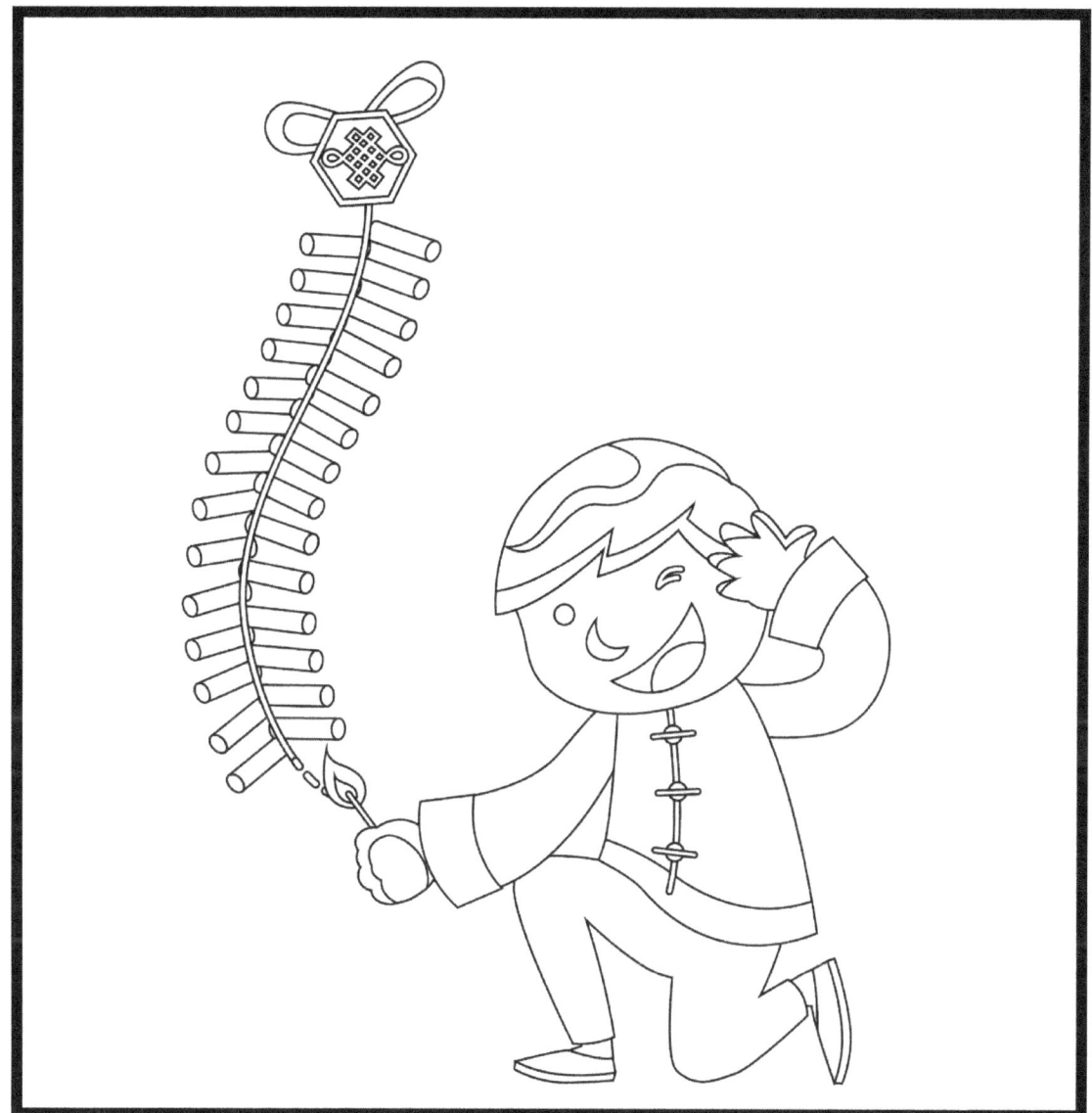

note:

_____

_____

_____

# SEPTEMBER 22TH

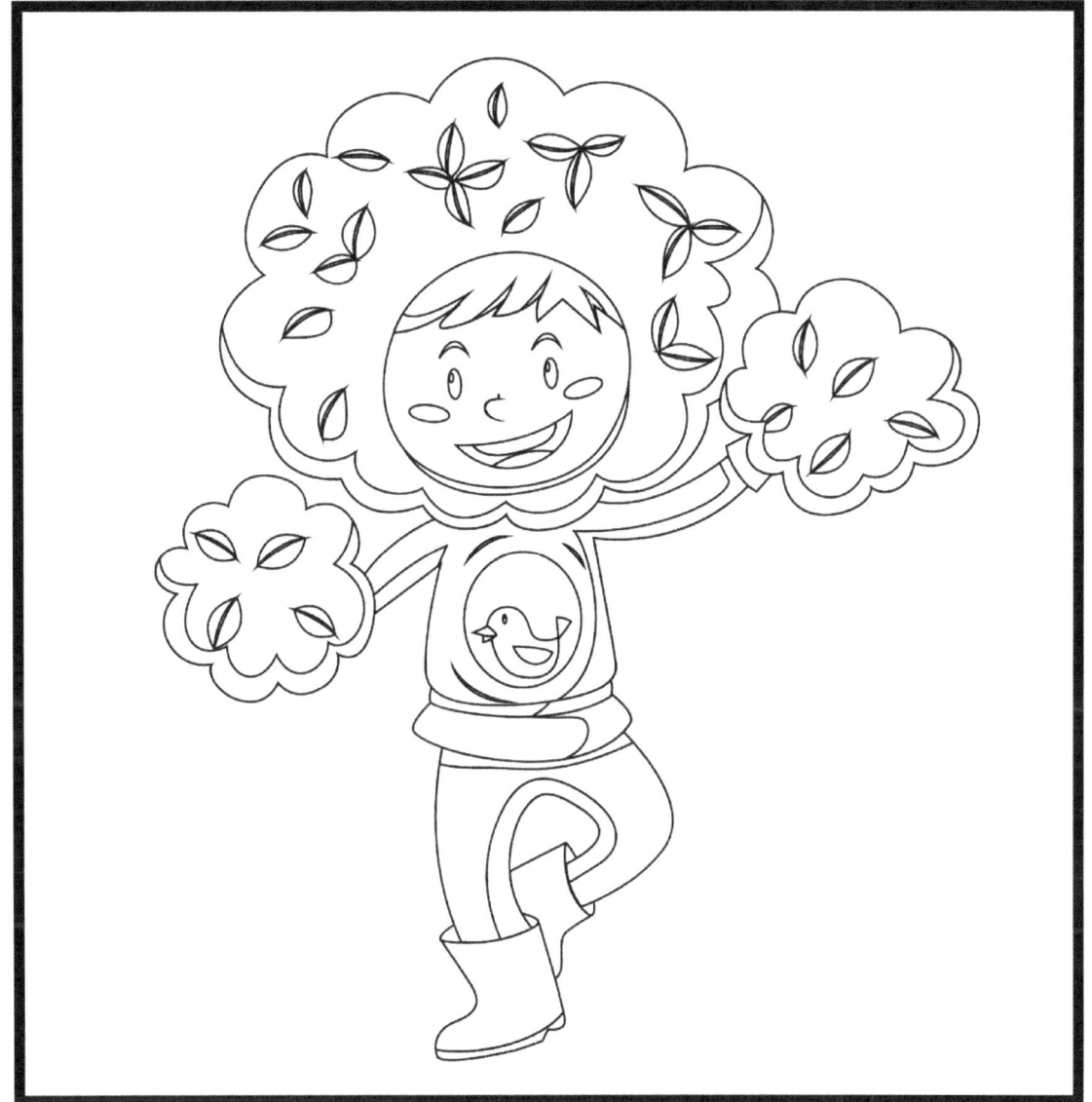

note:

_____

_____

_____

# SEPTEMBER 23TH

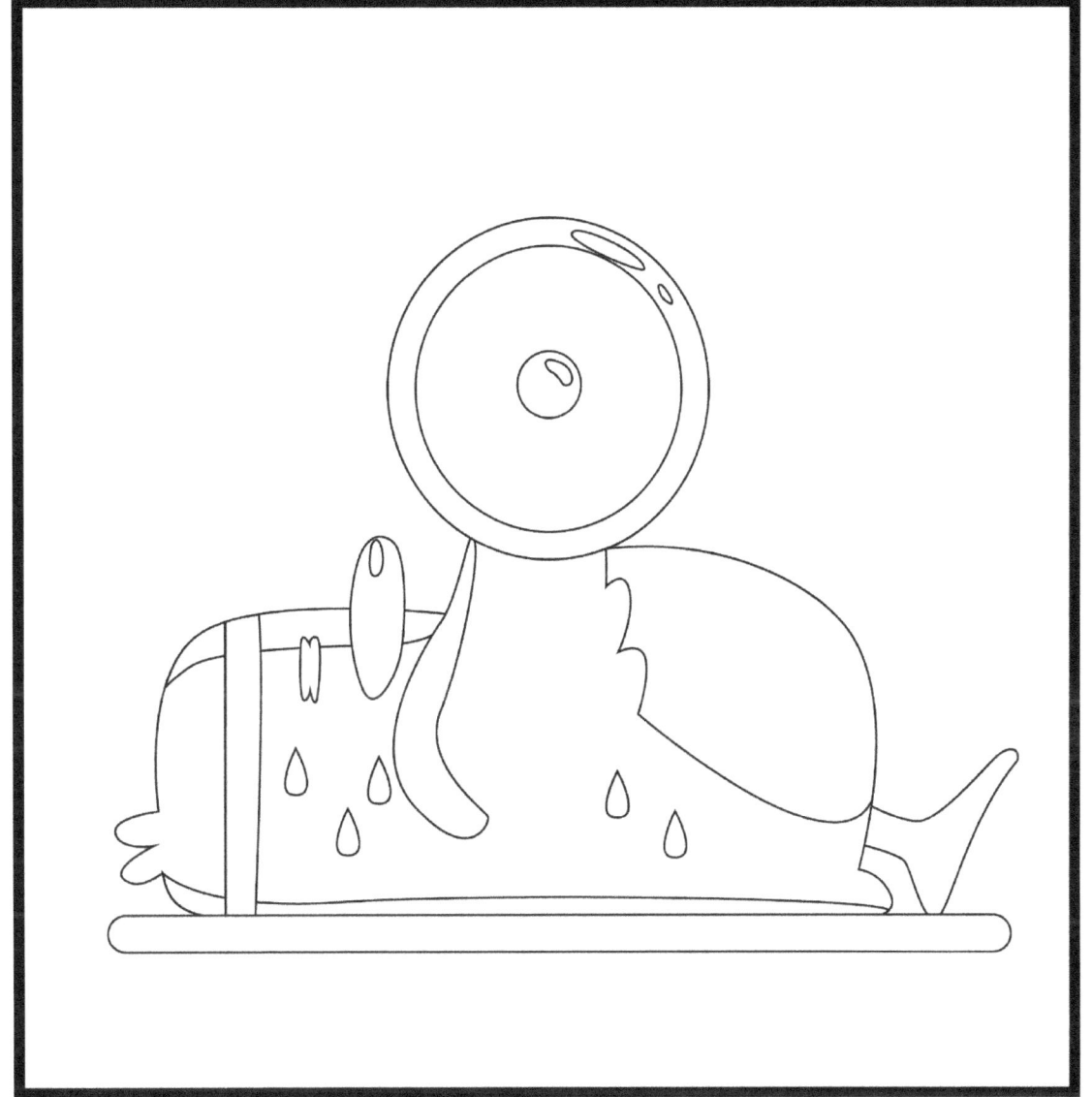

note:

_____

_____

_____

# SEPTEMBER 24TH

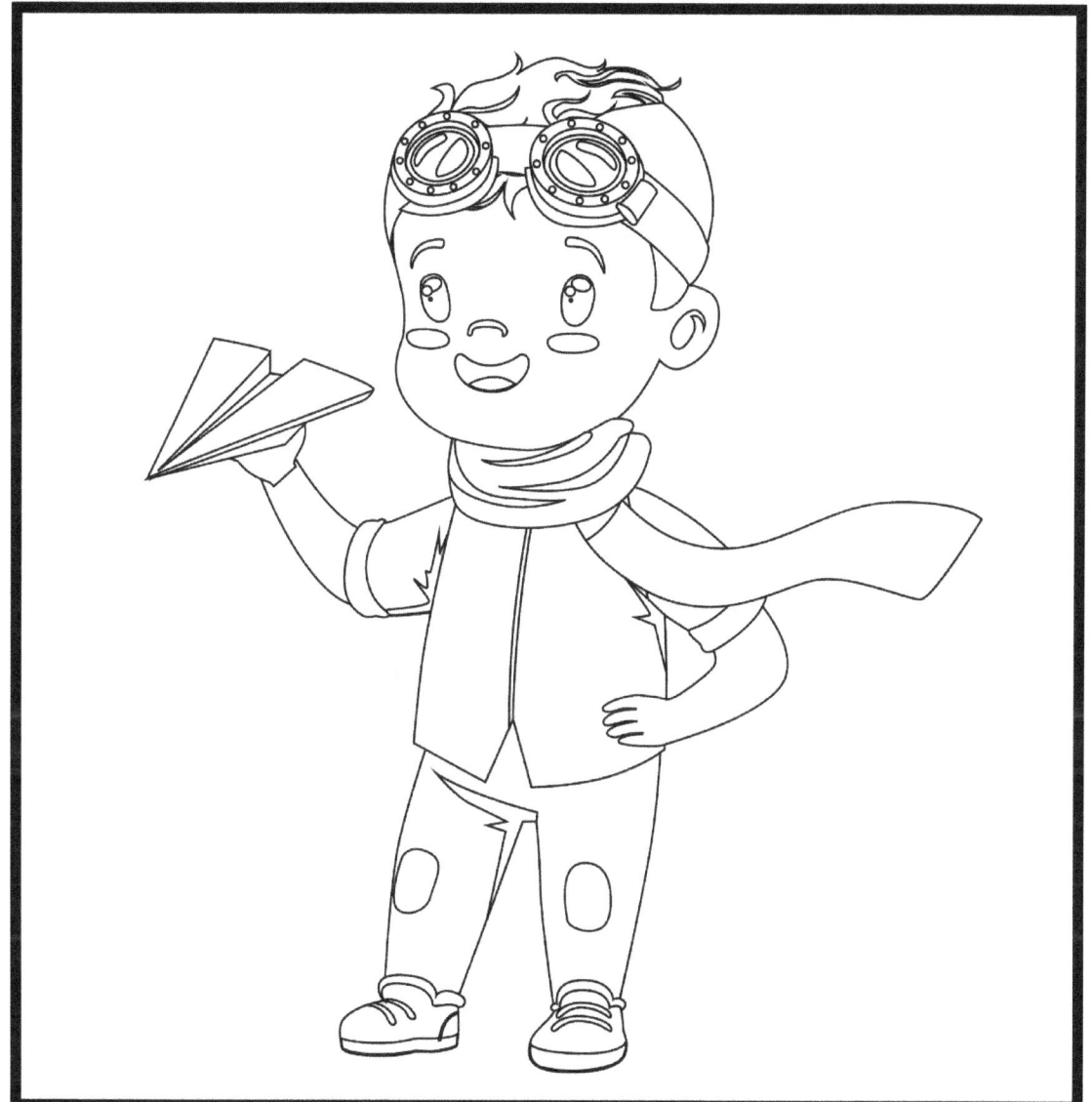

note:

_____

_____

_____

# SEPTEMBER 25TH

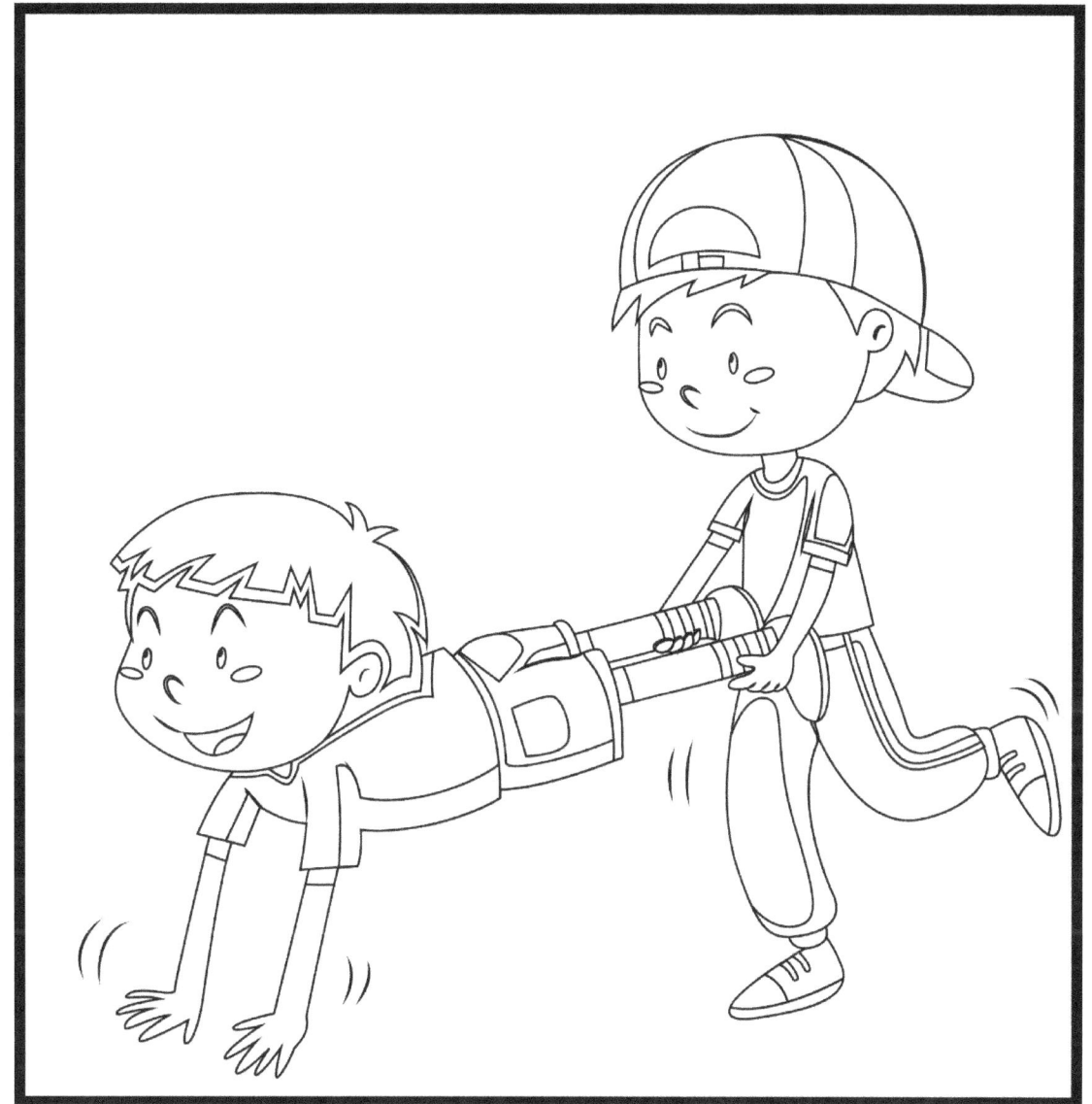

note:

_____

_____

_____

# SEPTEMBER 26TH

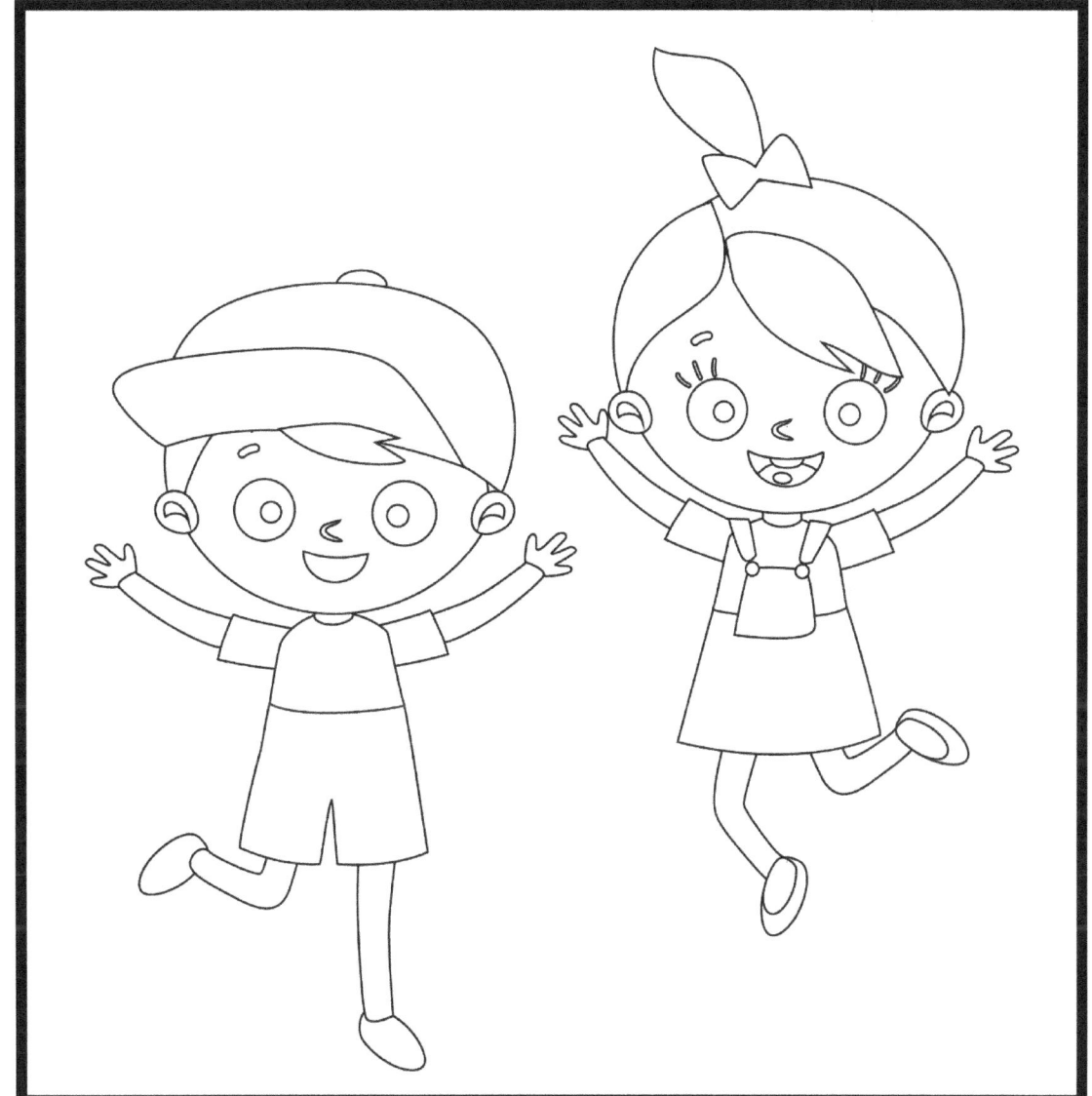

note:

_____

_____

_____

# SEPTEMBER 27TH

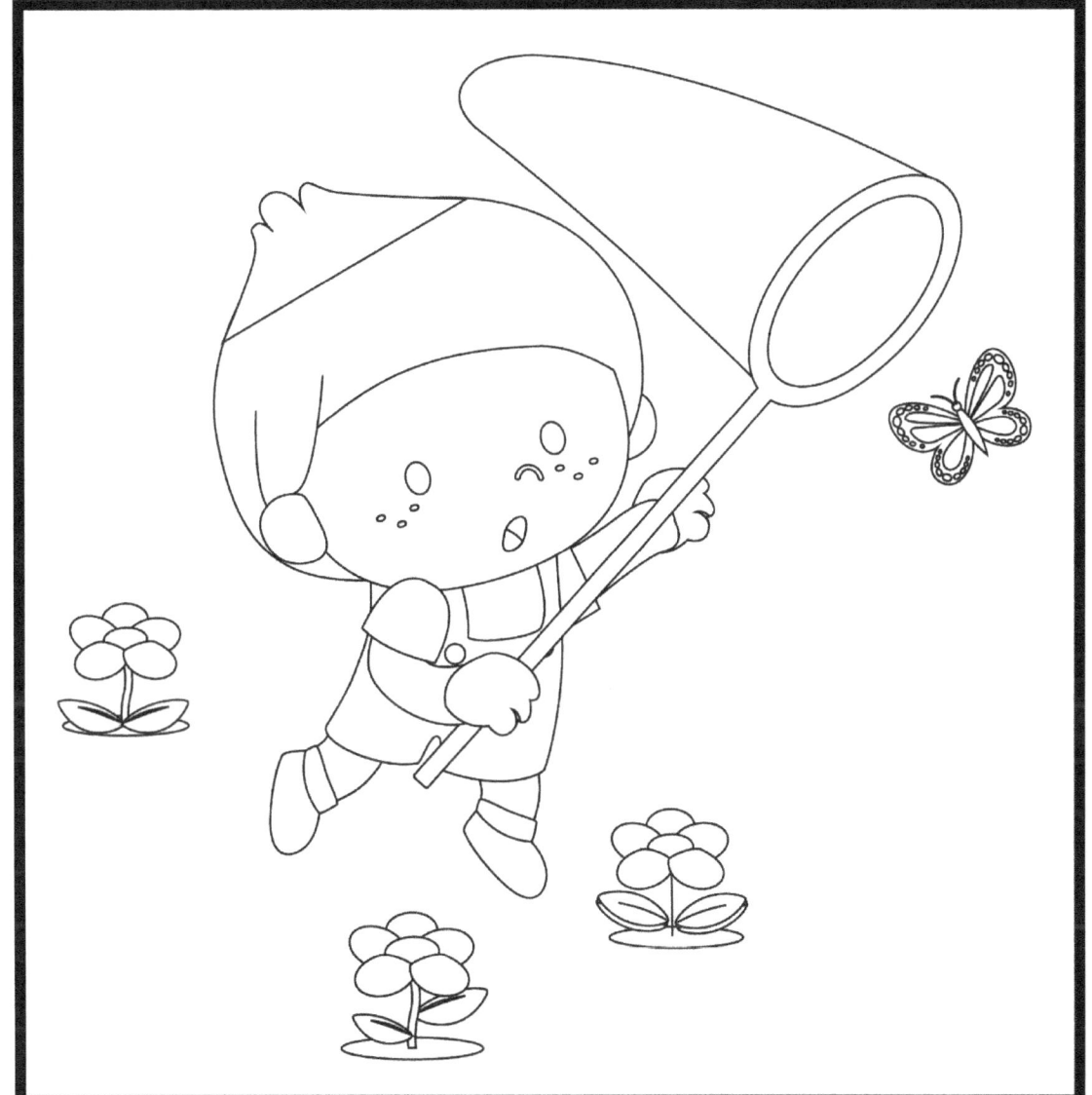

note:

_____

_____

_____

# SEPTEMBER 28TH

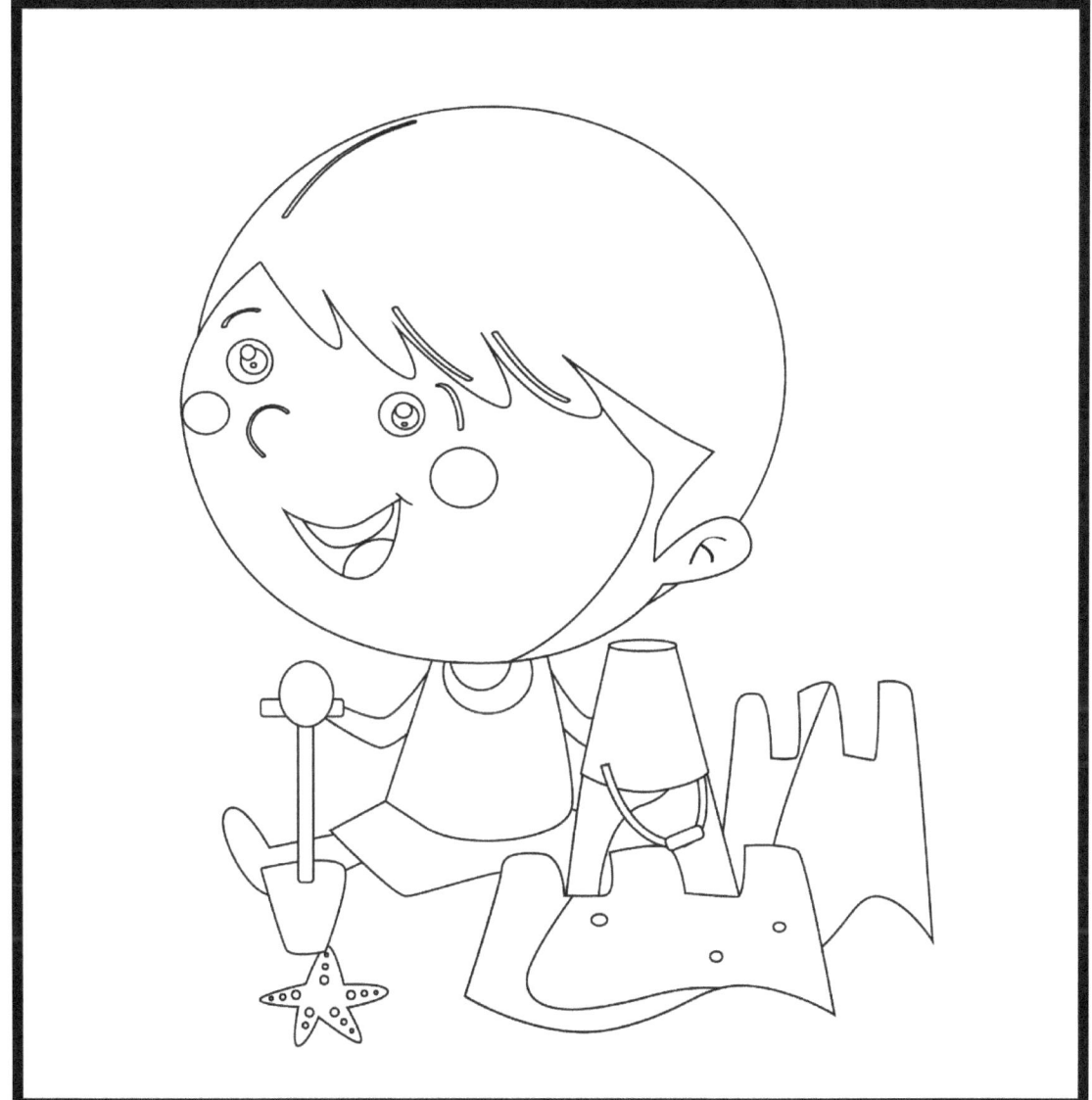

note:

_____

_____

_____

# SEPTEMBER 29TH

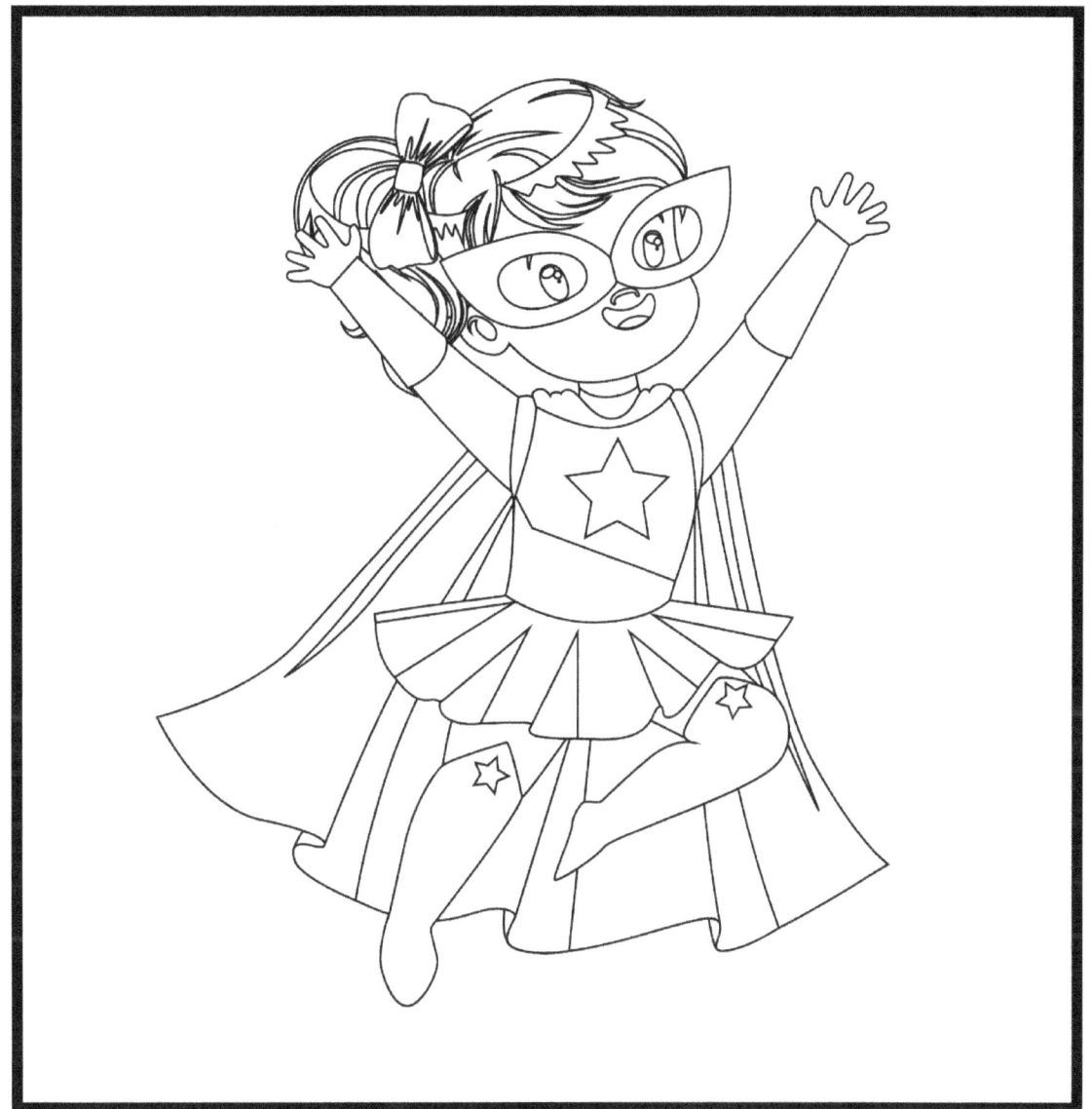

note:

_____

_____

_____

# SEPTEMBER 30TH

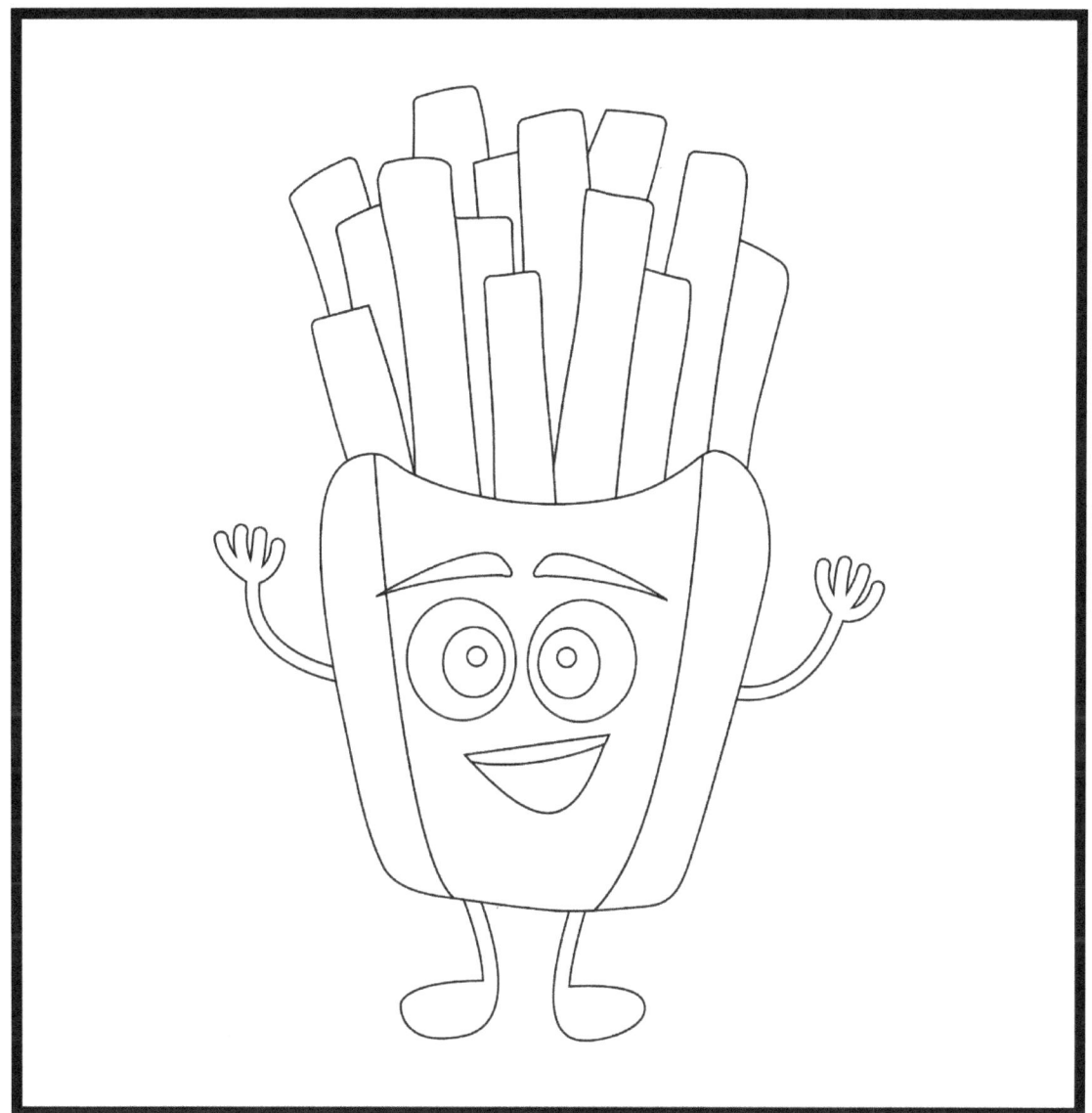

note:

_____

_____

_____

# SEPTEMBER 31TH

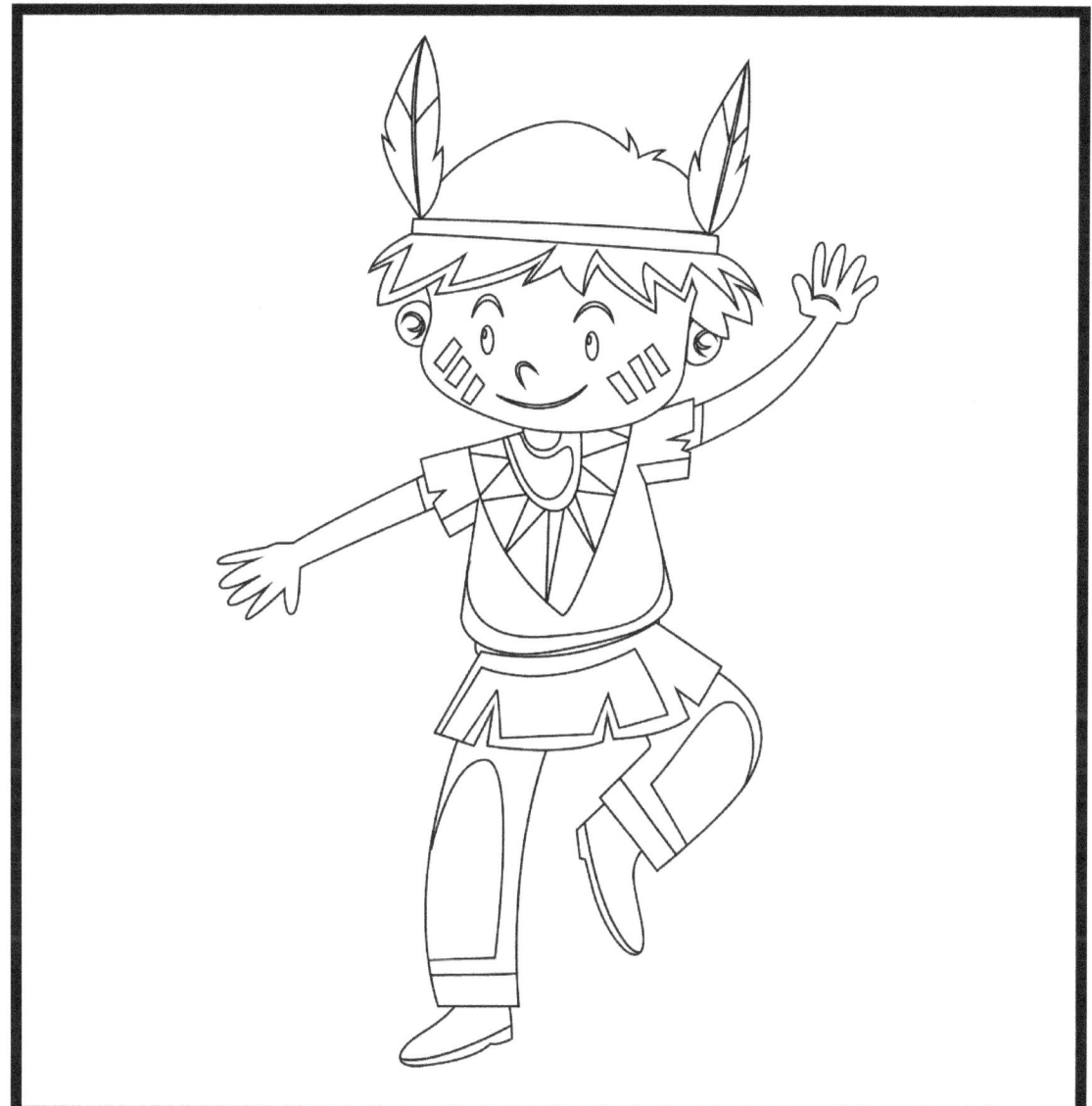

note:

_____

_____

_____

# SEPTEMBER 32TH

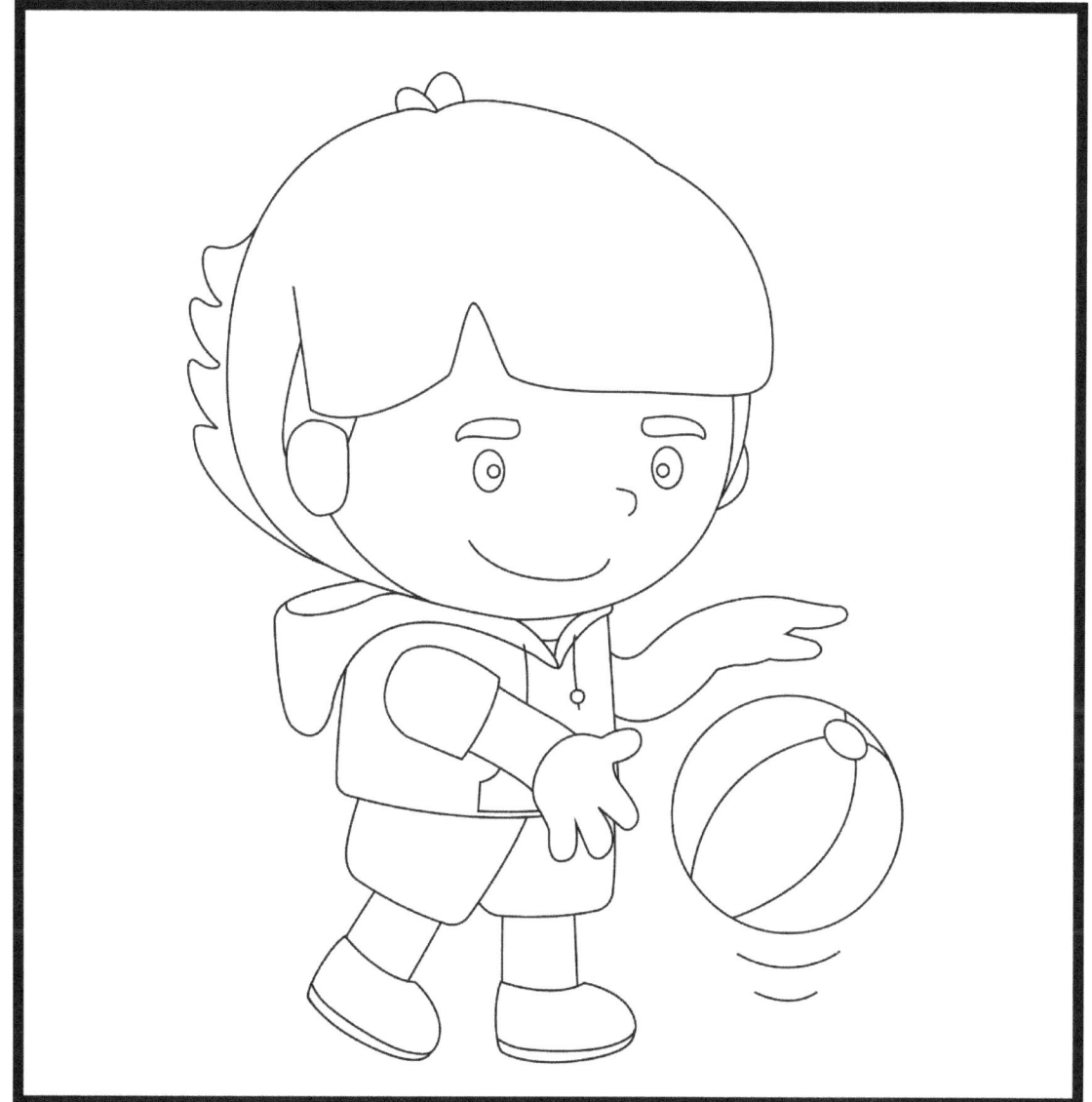

note:

_____

_____

_____

# SEPTEMBER 33TH

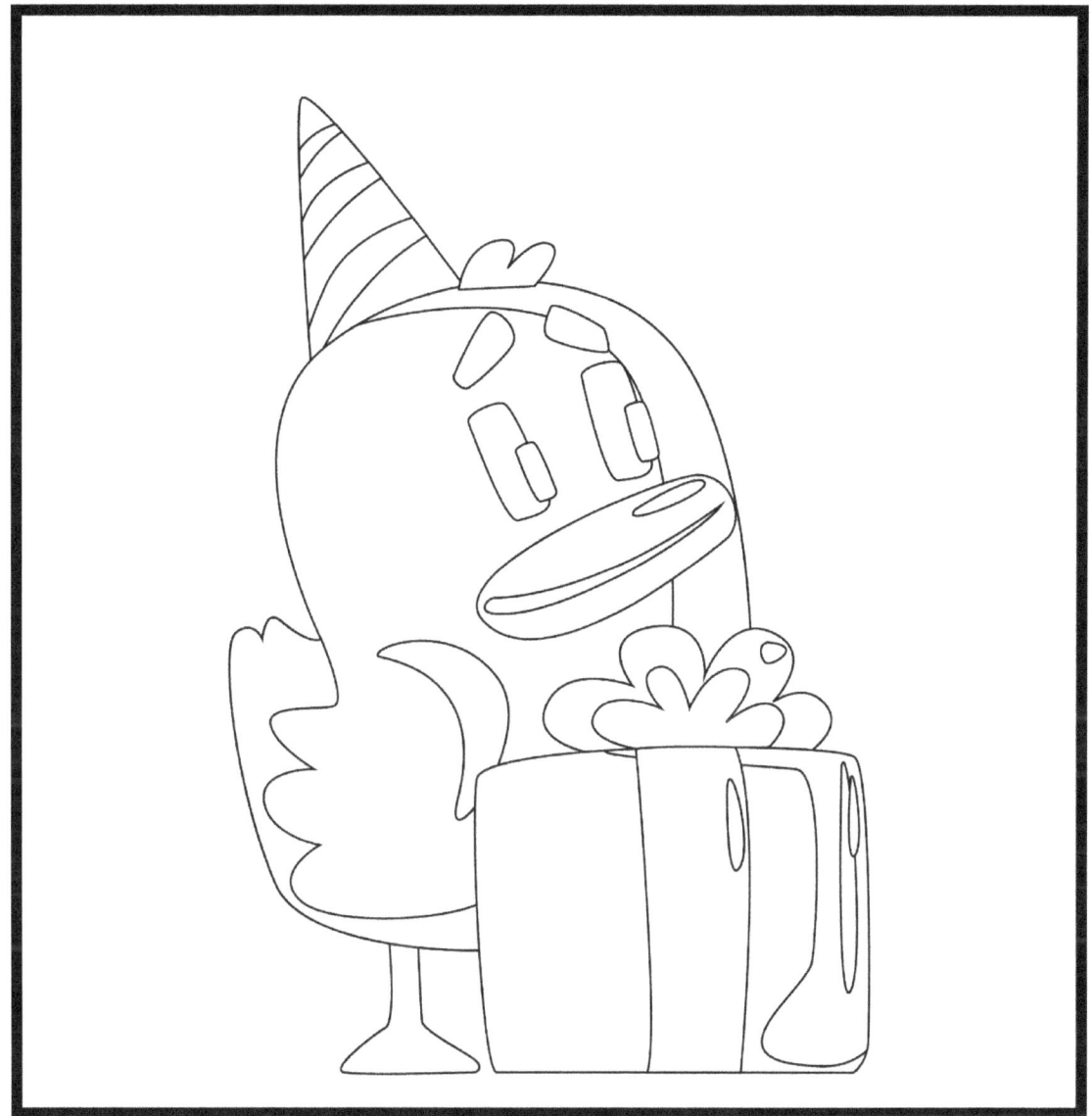

note:

_____

_____

_____

# SEPTEMBER 34TH

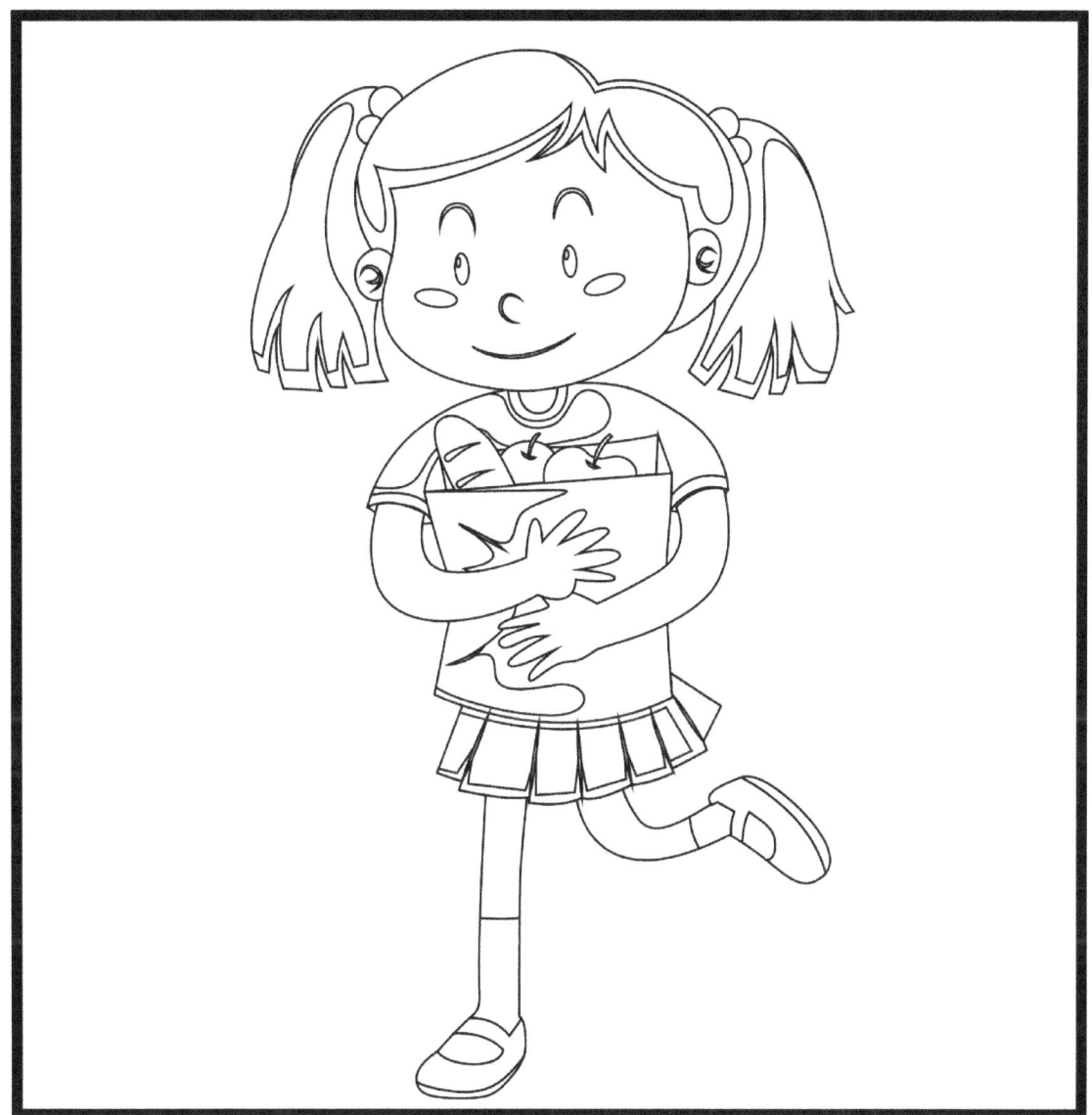

note:

_____

_____

_____

# SEPTEMBER 35TH

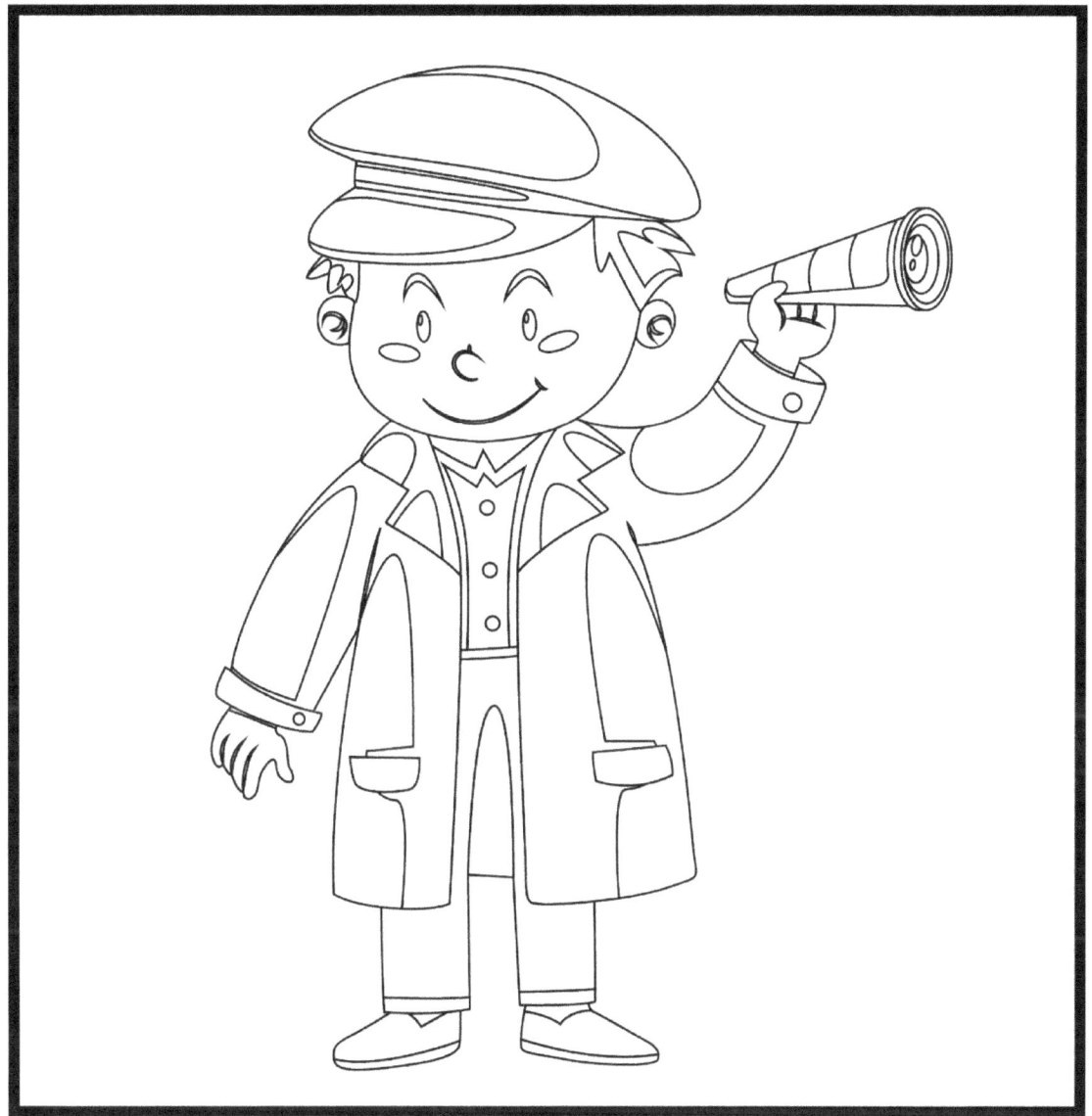

note:

_____

_____

_____

# SEPTEMBER 36TH

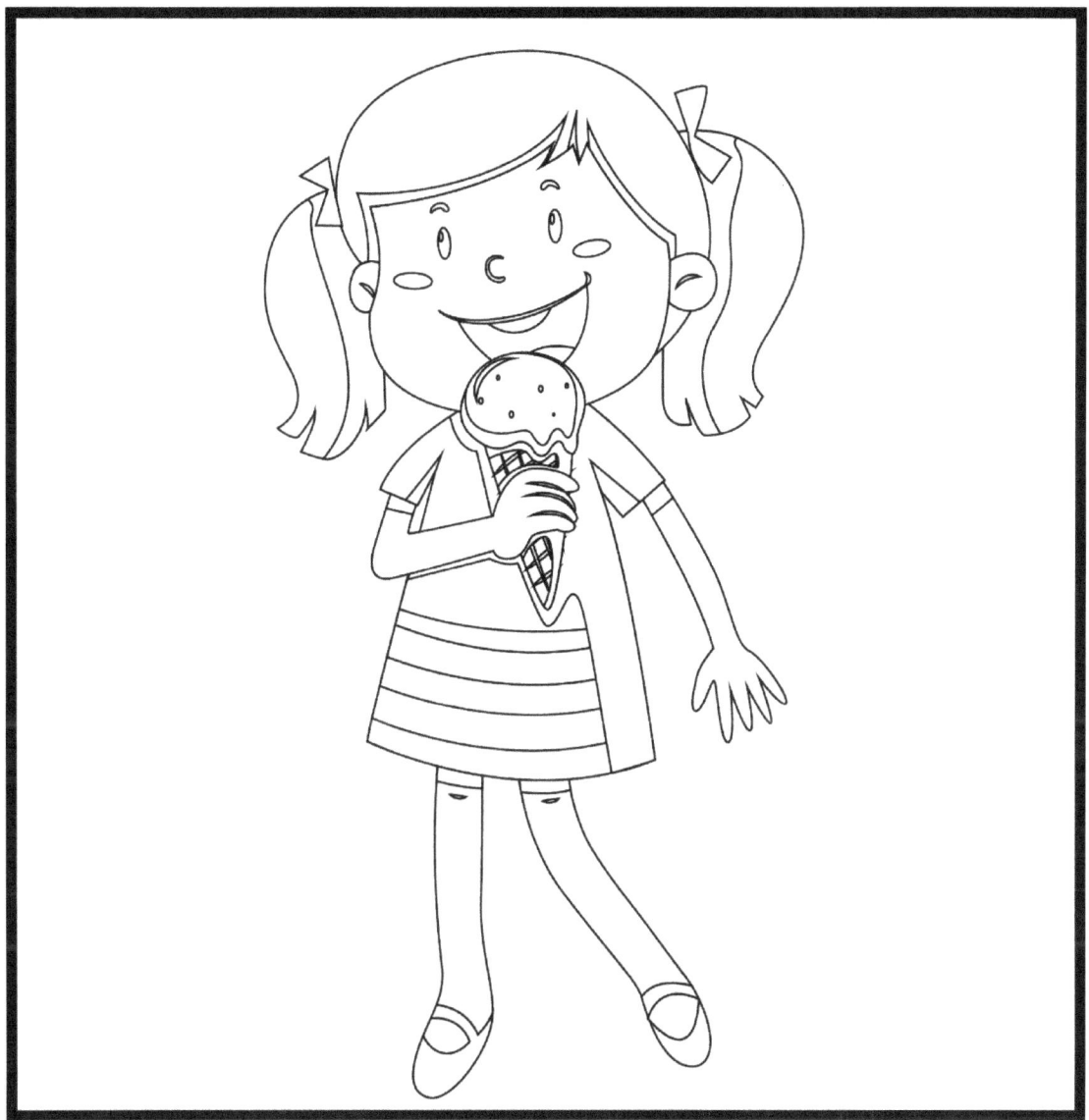

note:

_____

_____

_____

# SEPTEMBER 37TH

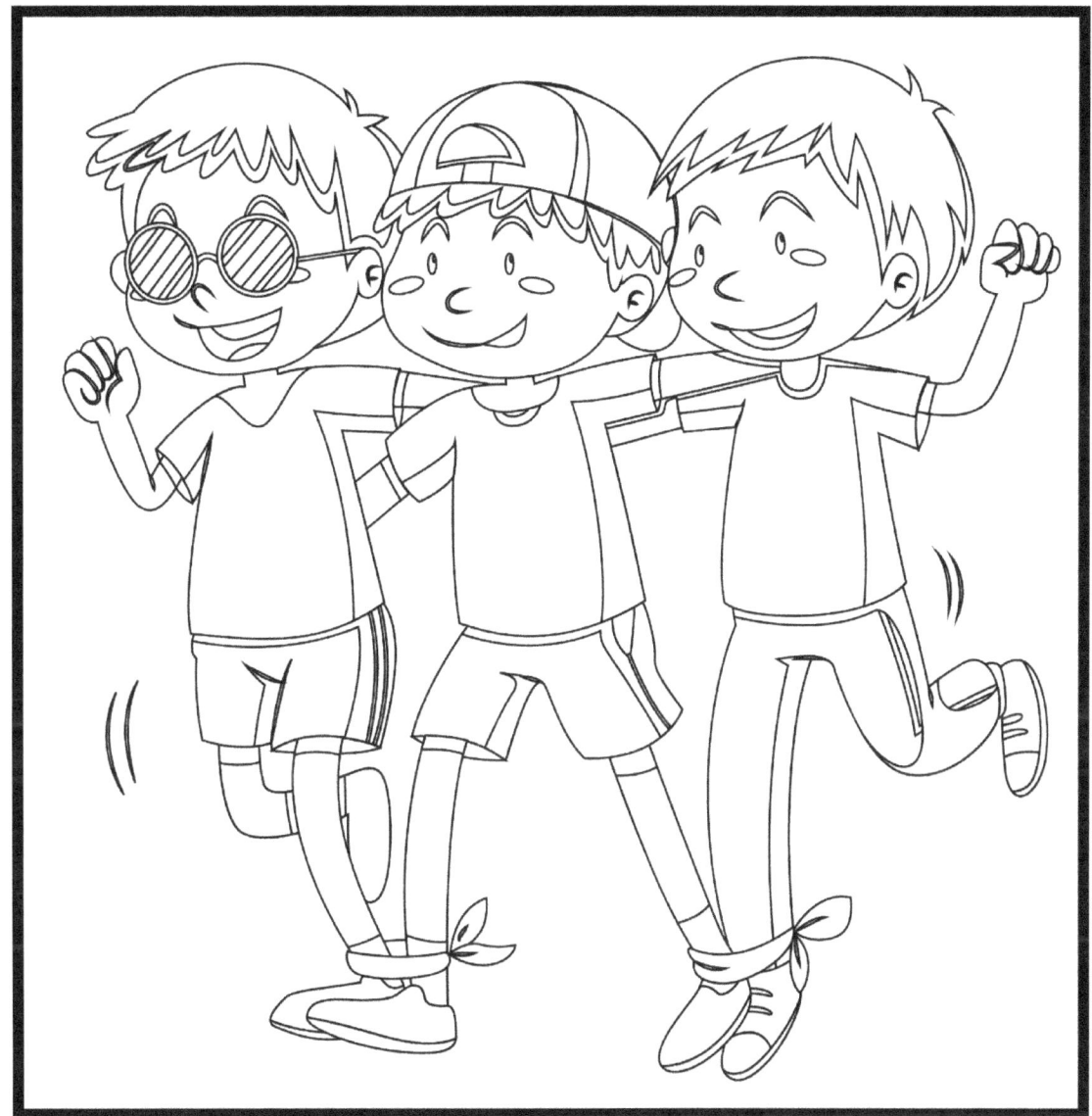

note:

_____

_____

_____

# SEPTEMBER 38TH

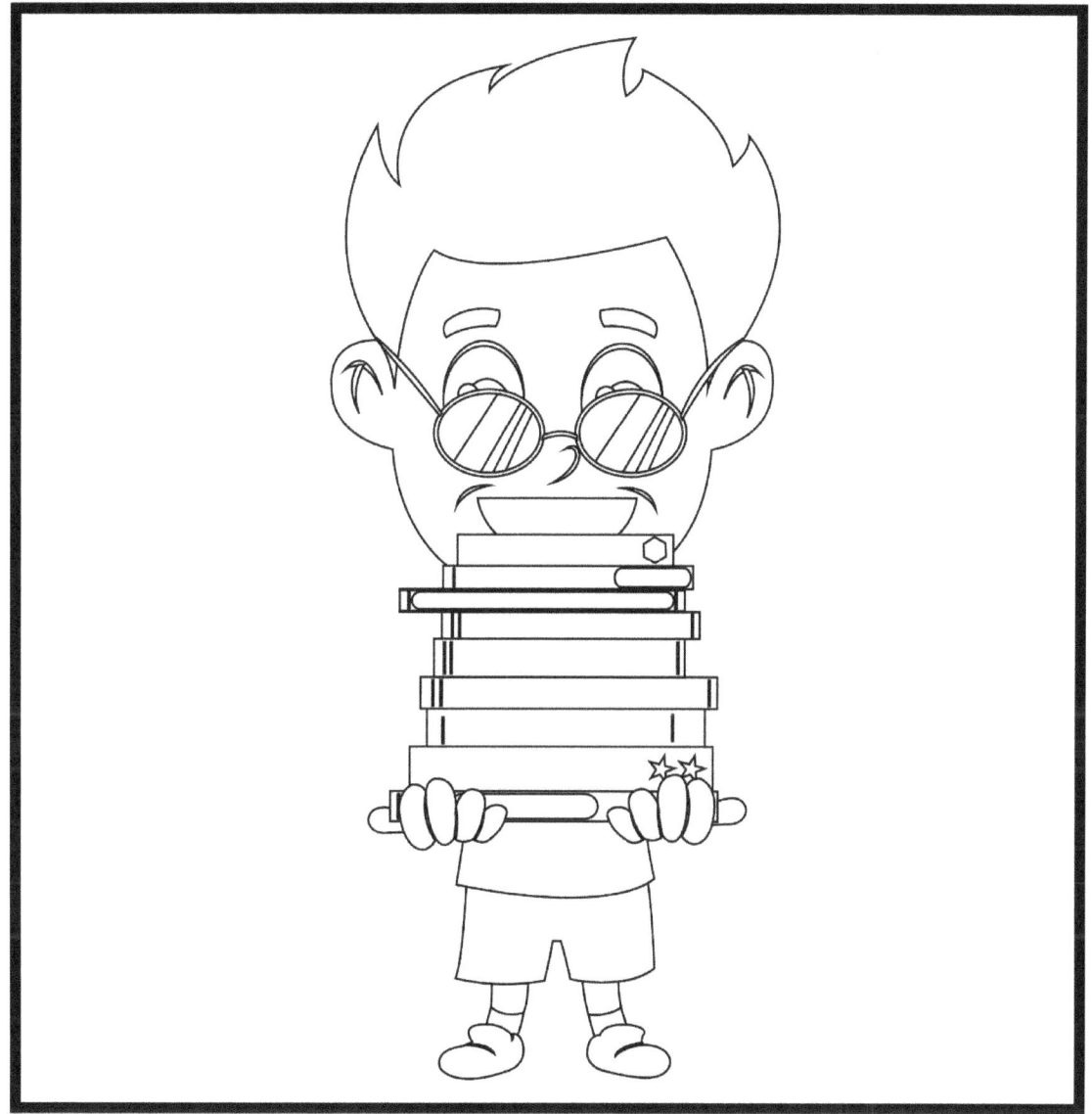

note:

_____

_____

_____

# SEPTEMBER 39TH

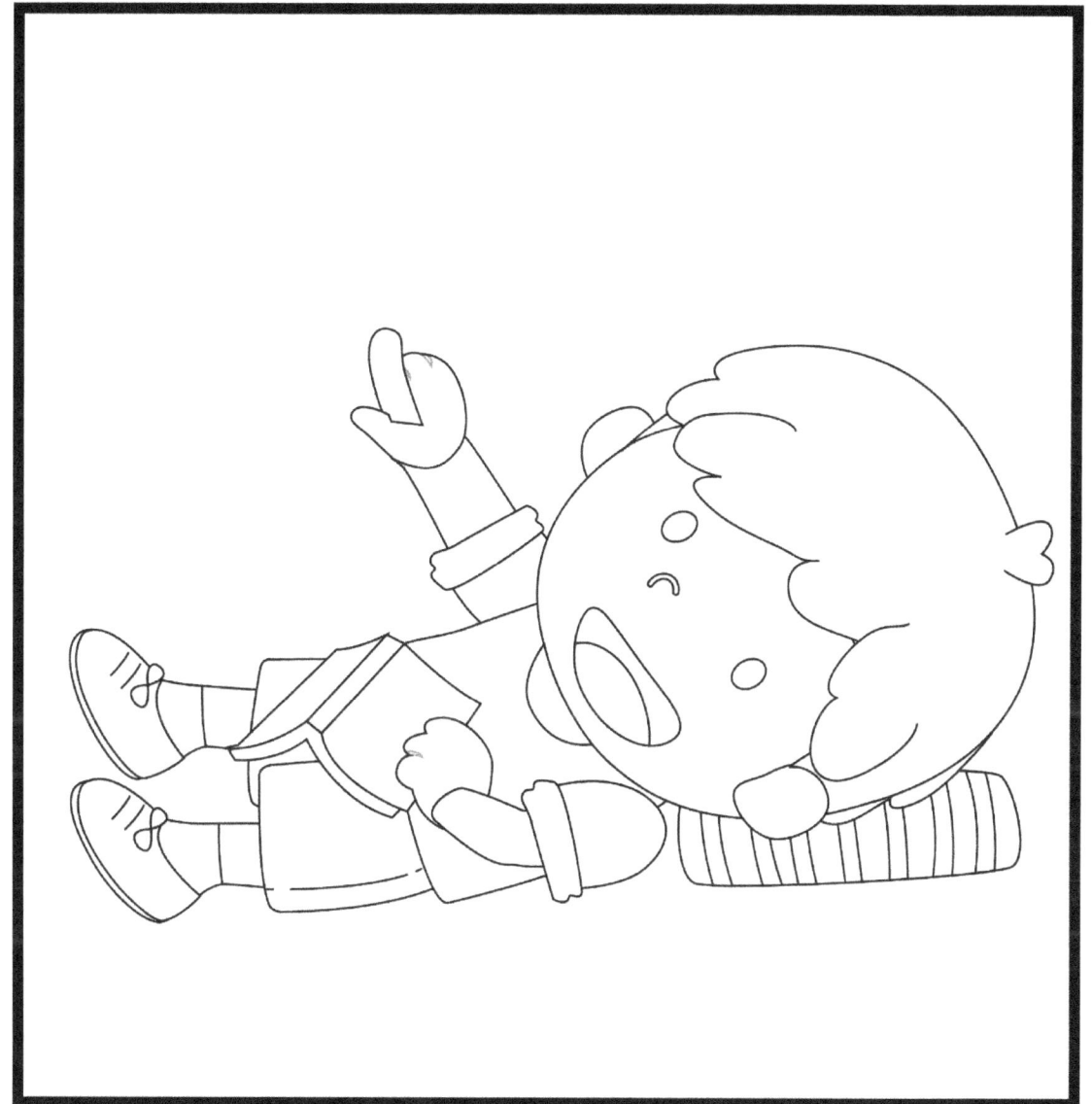

note:

_____

_____

_____

# SEPTEMBER 40TH

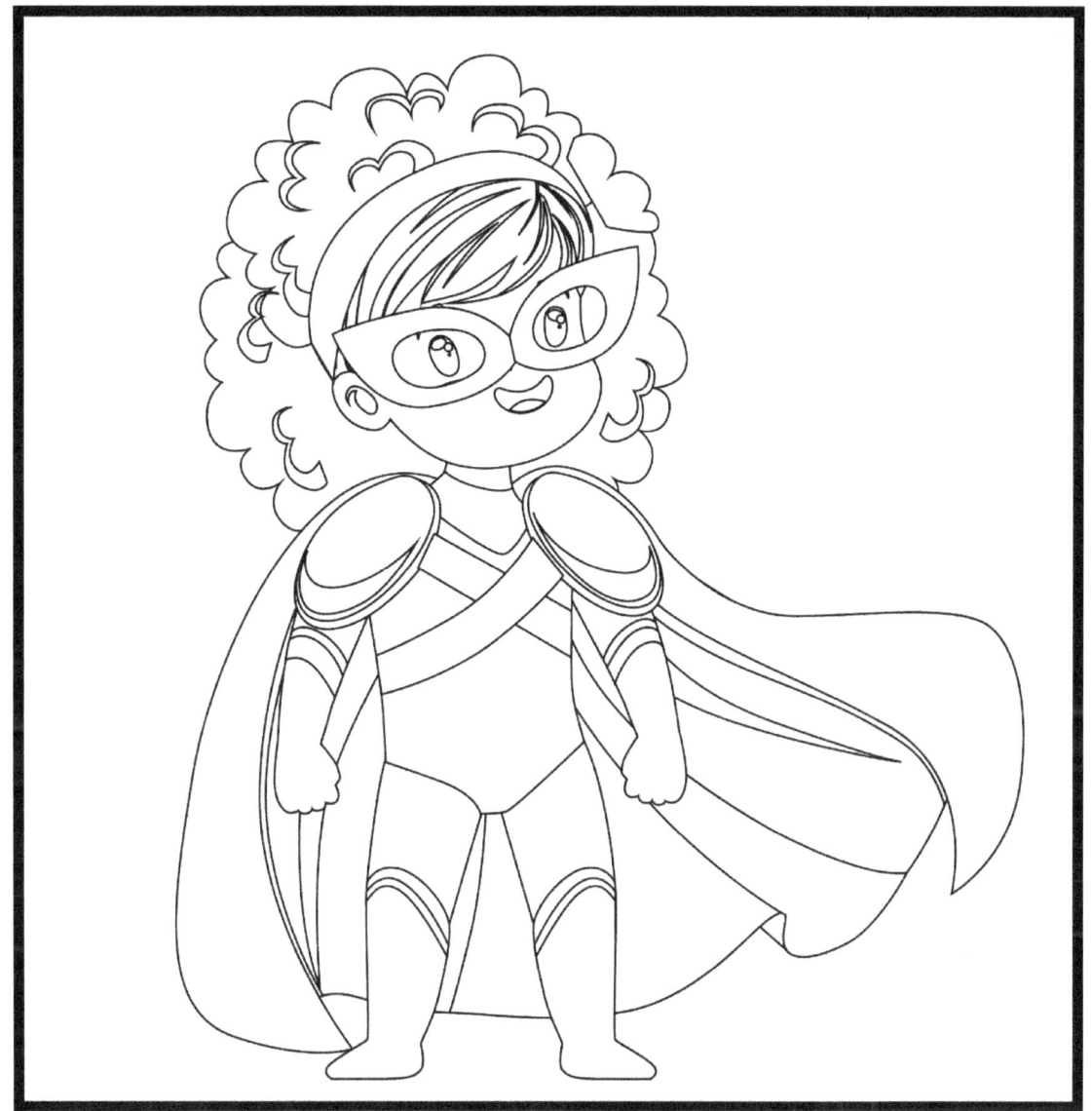

note:

_____

_____

_____

# SEPTEMBER 41TH

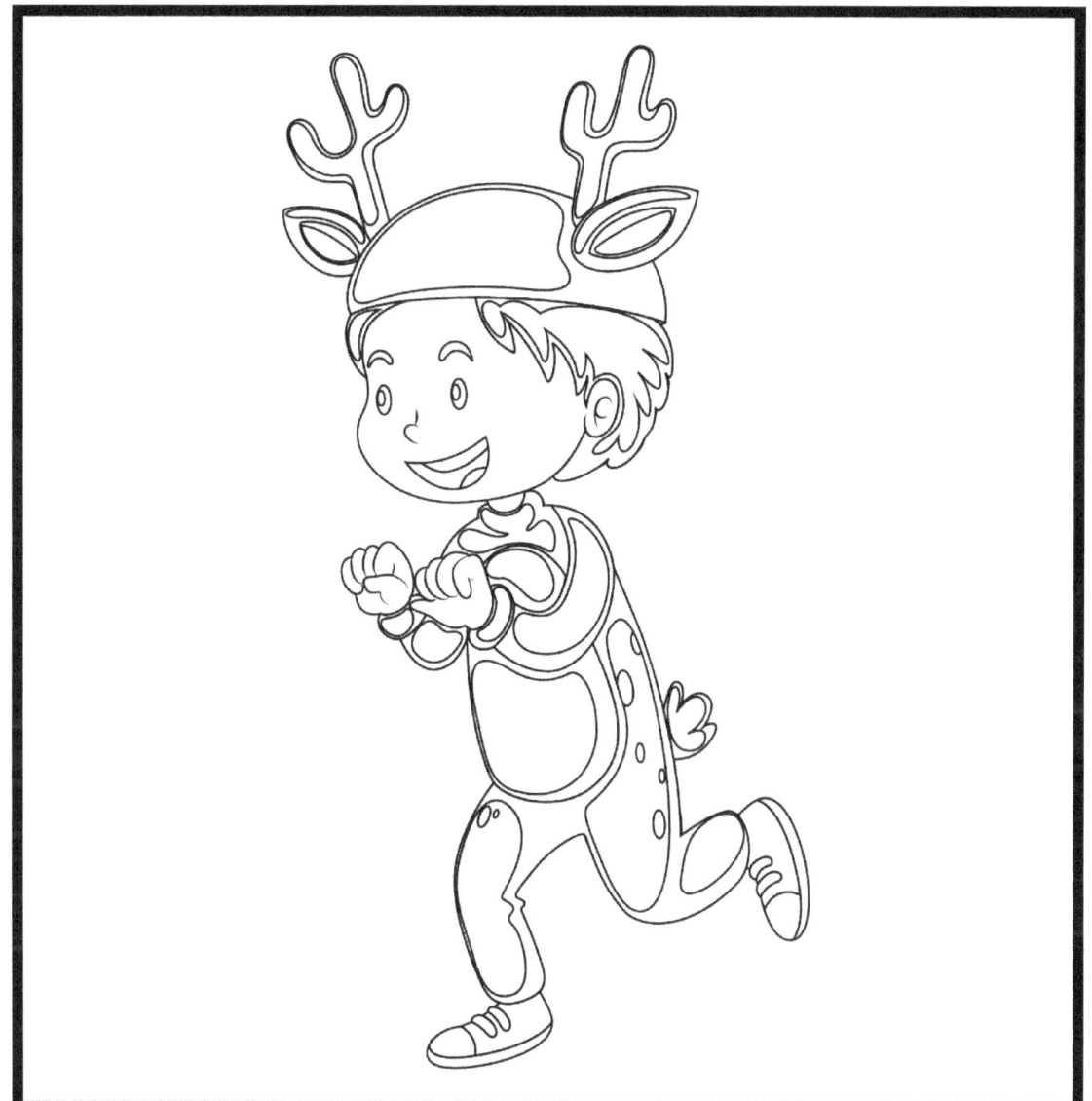

note:

_____

_____

_____

# SEPTEMBER 42TH

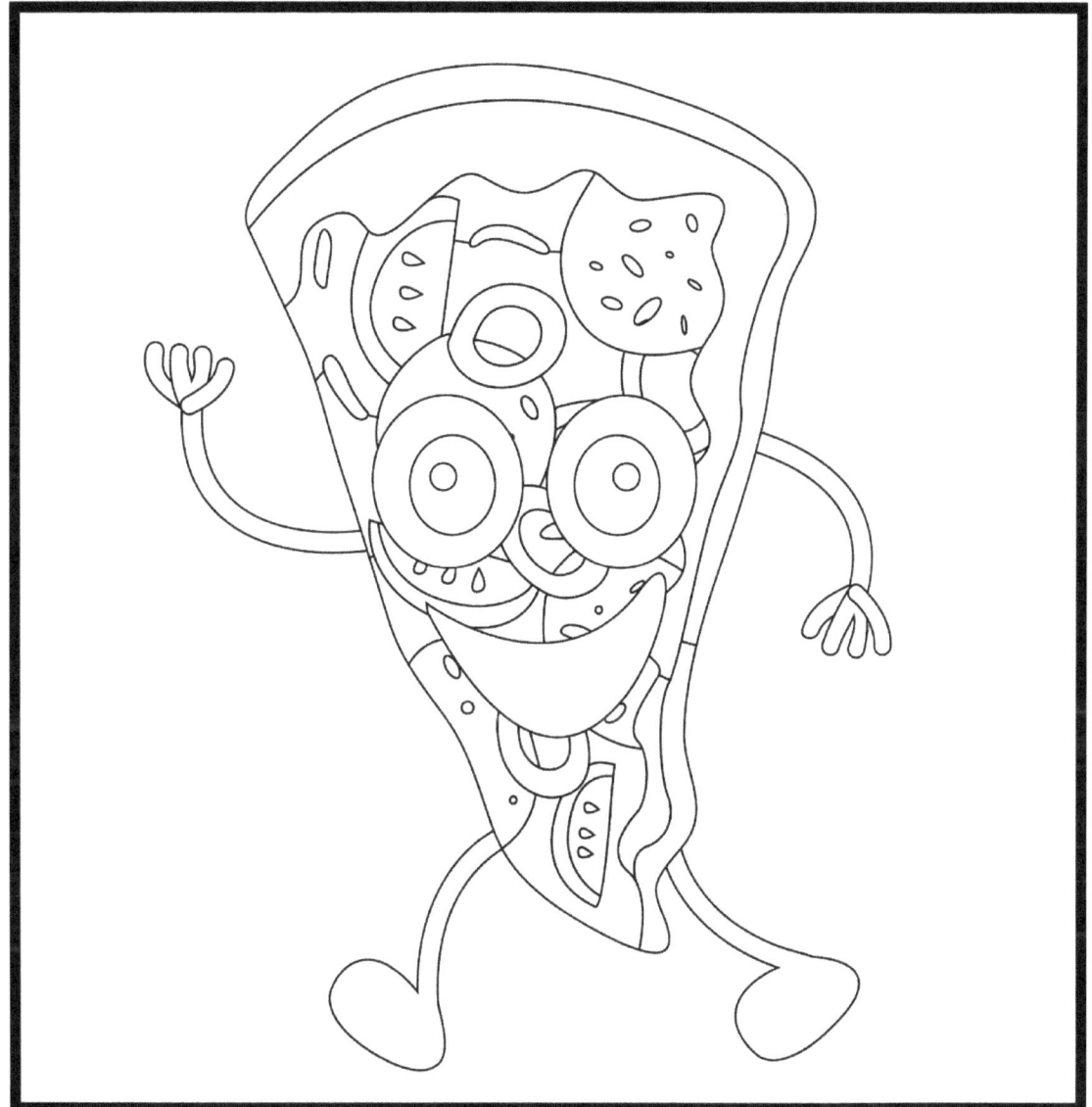

note:

_____

_____

_____

# SEPTEMBER 43TH

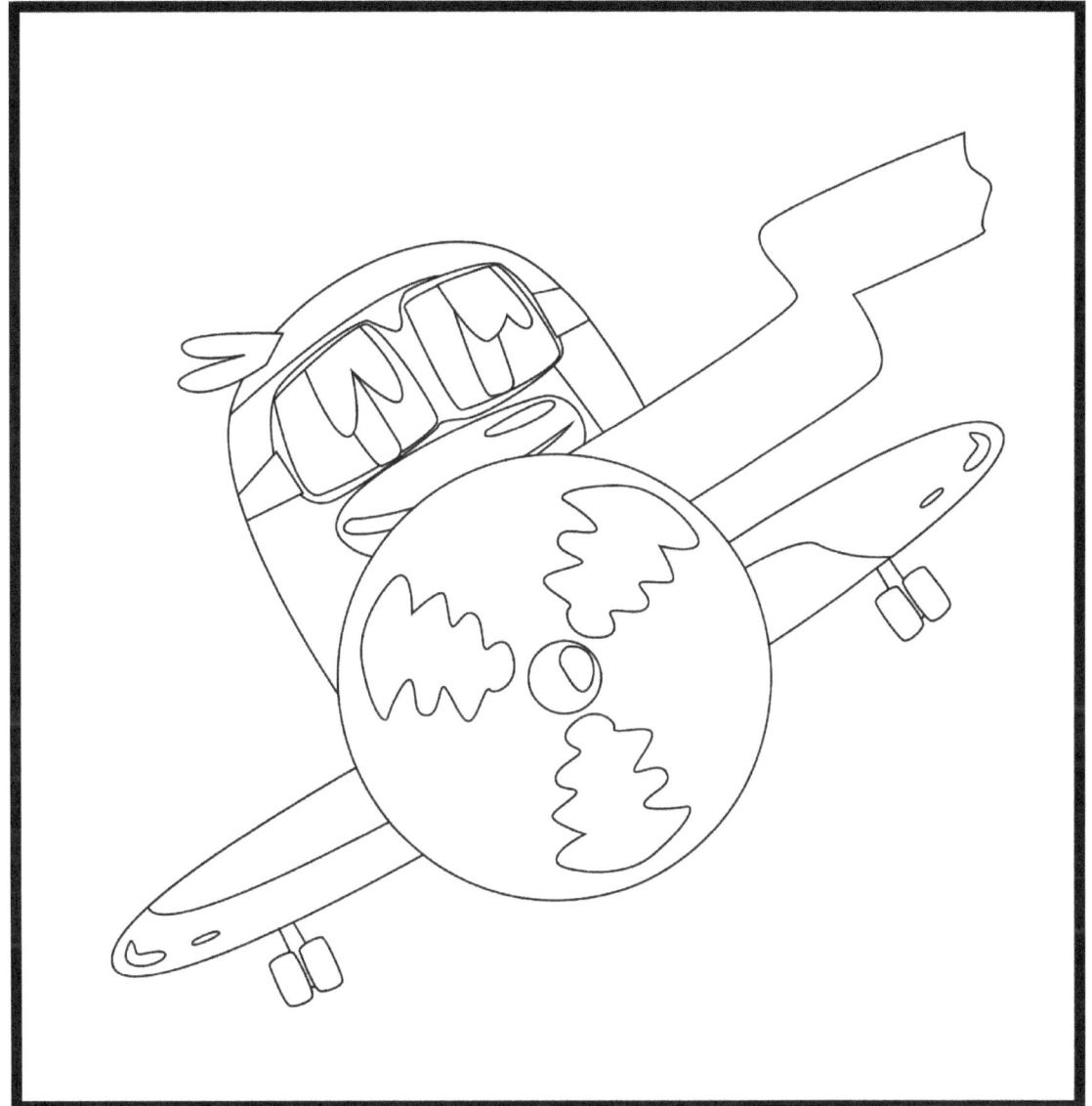

note:

_____

_____

_____

# SEPTEMBER 44TH

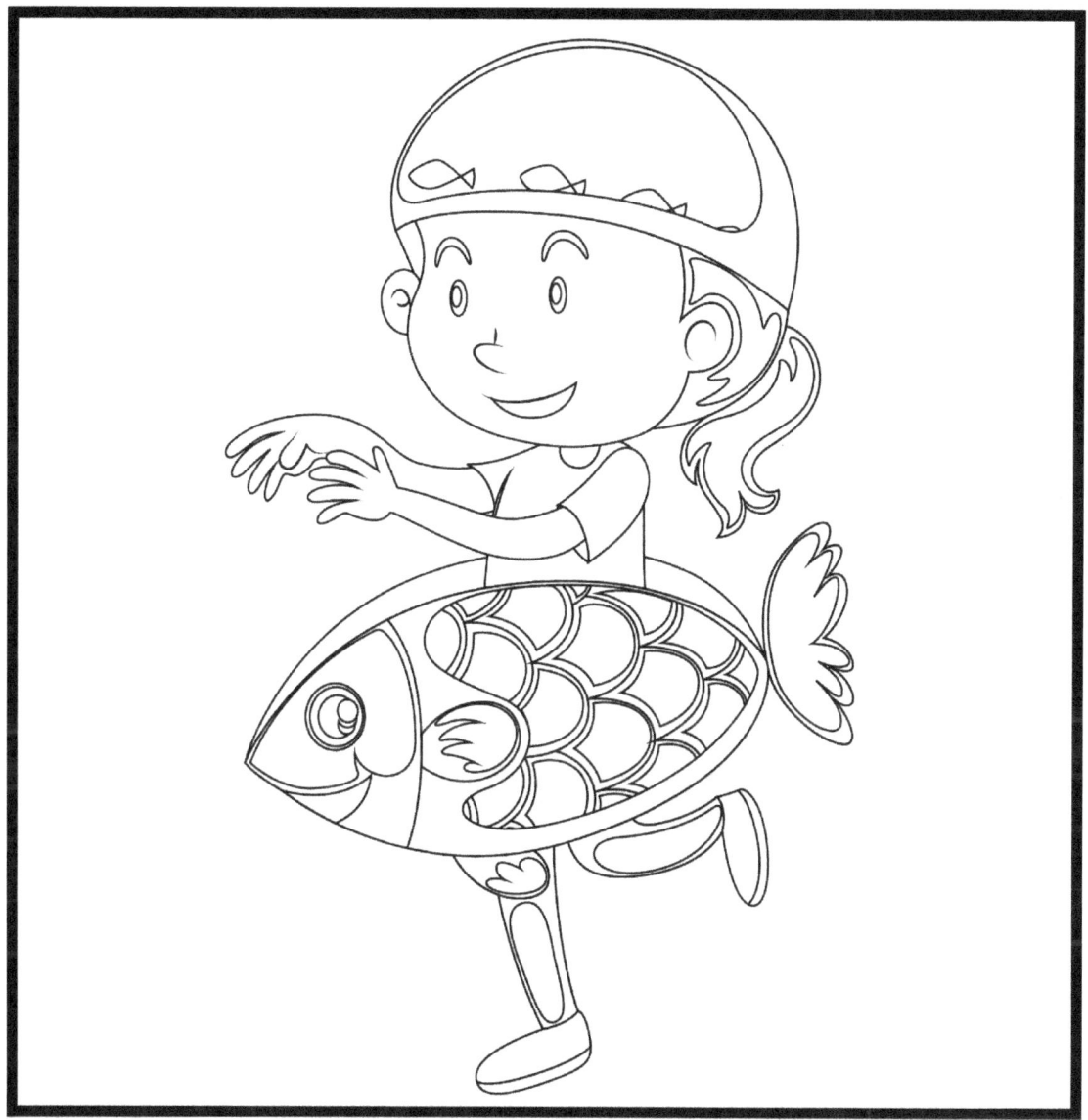

note:

_____

_____

_____

# SEPTEMBER 45TH

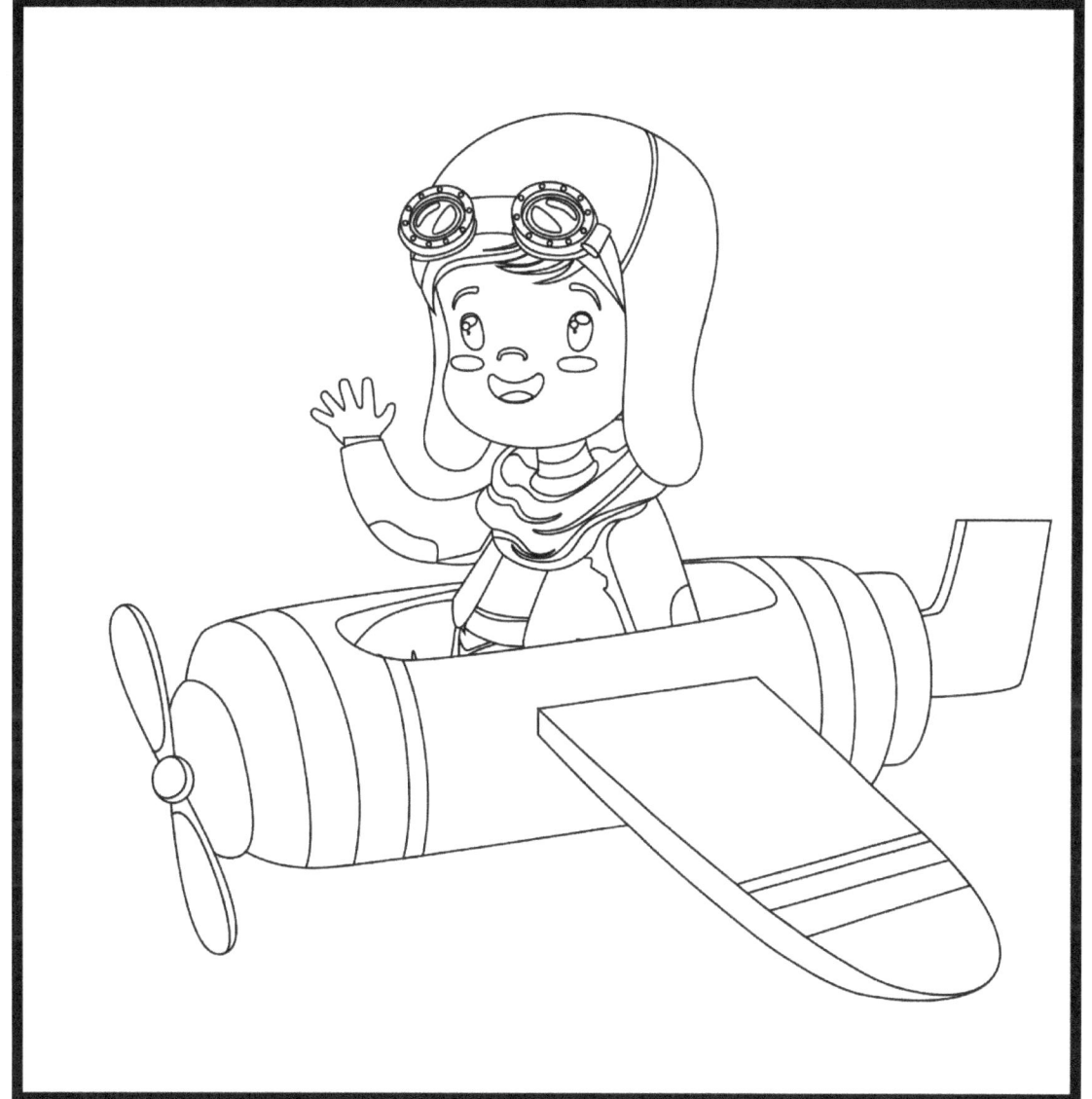

note:

_____

_____

_____

# SEPTEMBER 46TH

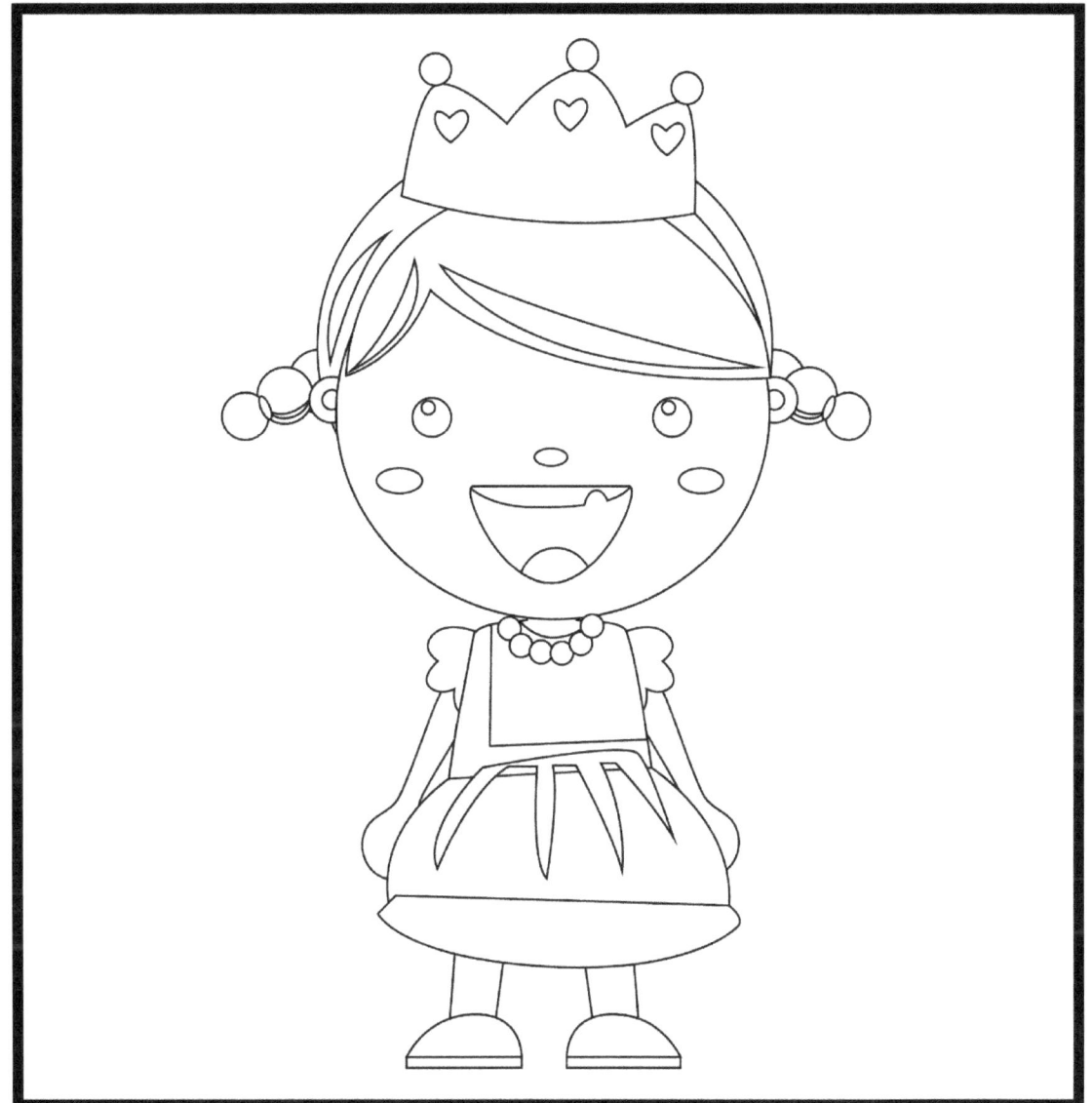

note:

_____

_____

_____

# SEPTEMBER 47TH

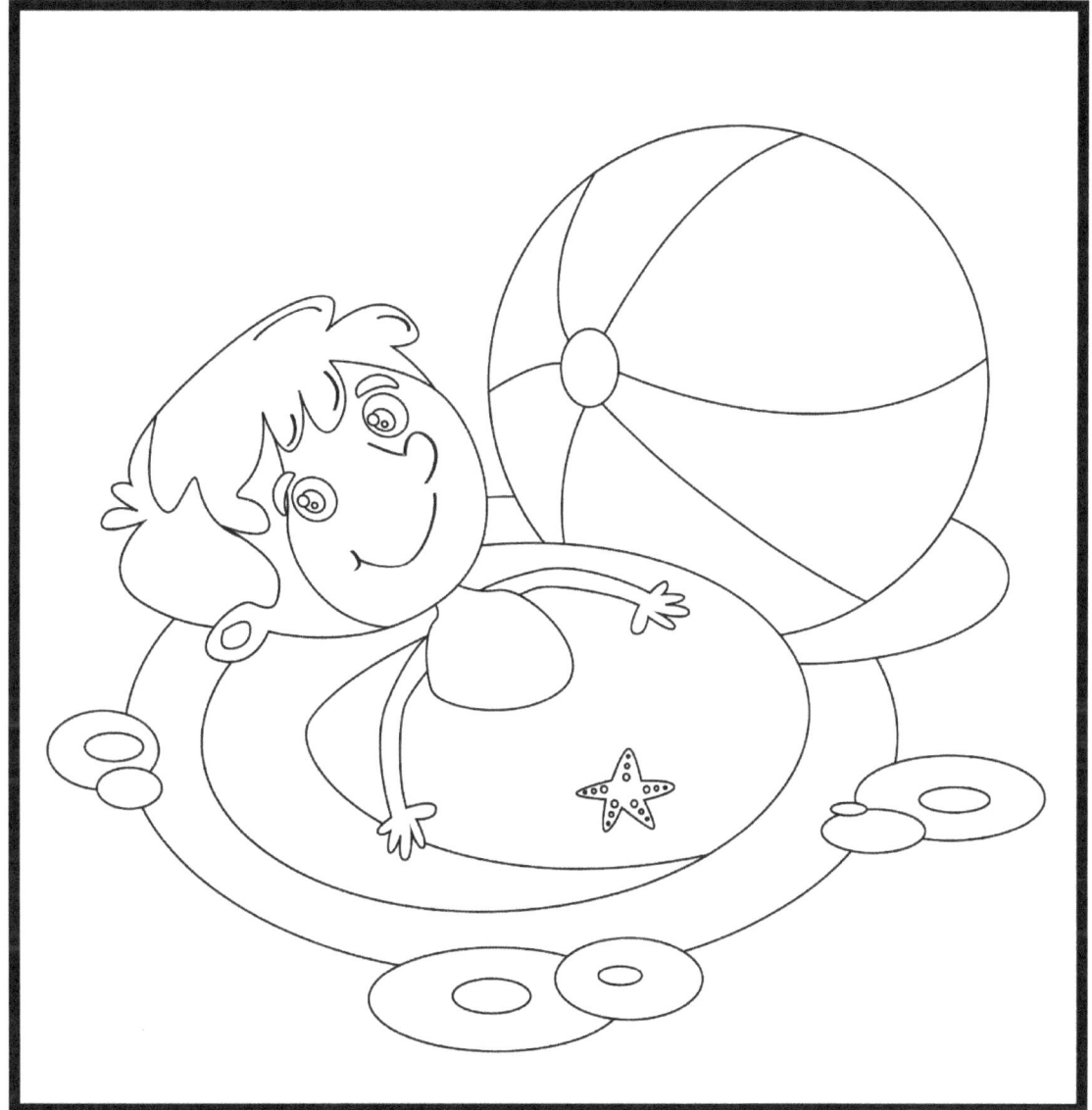

note:

_____

_____

_____

# SEPTEMBER 48TH

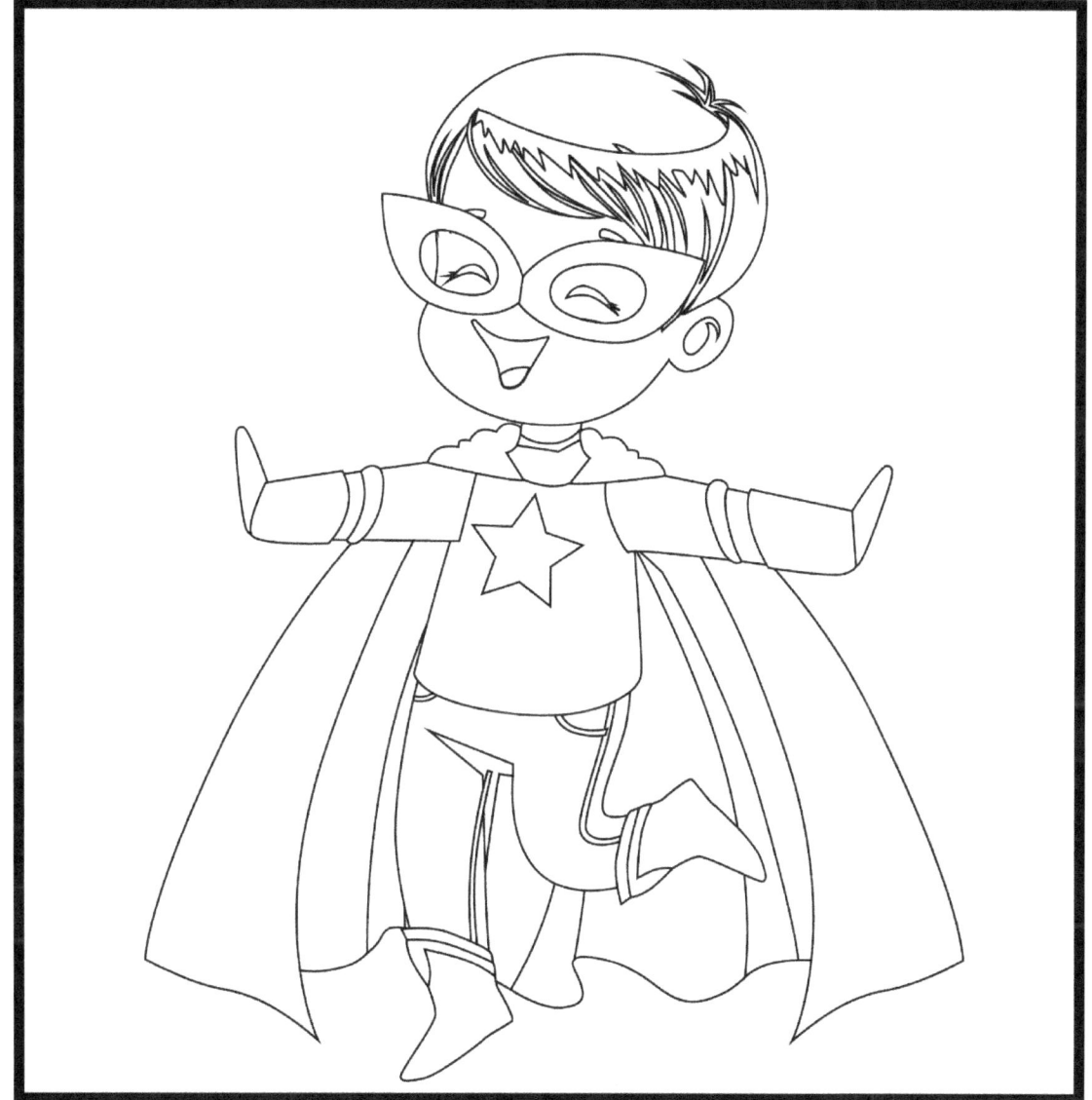

note:

_____

_____

_____

# SEPTEMBER 49TH

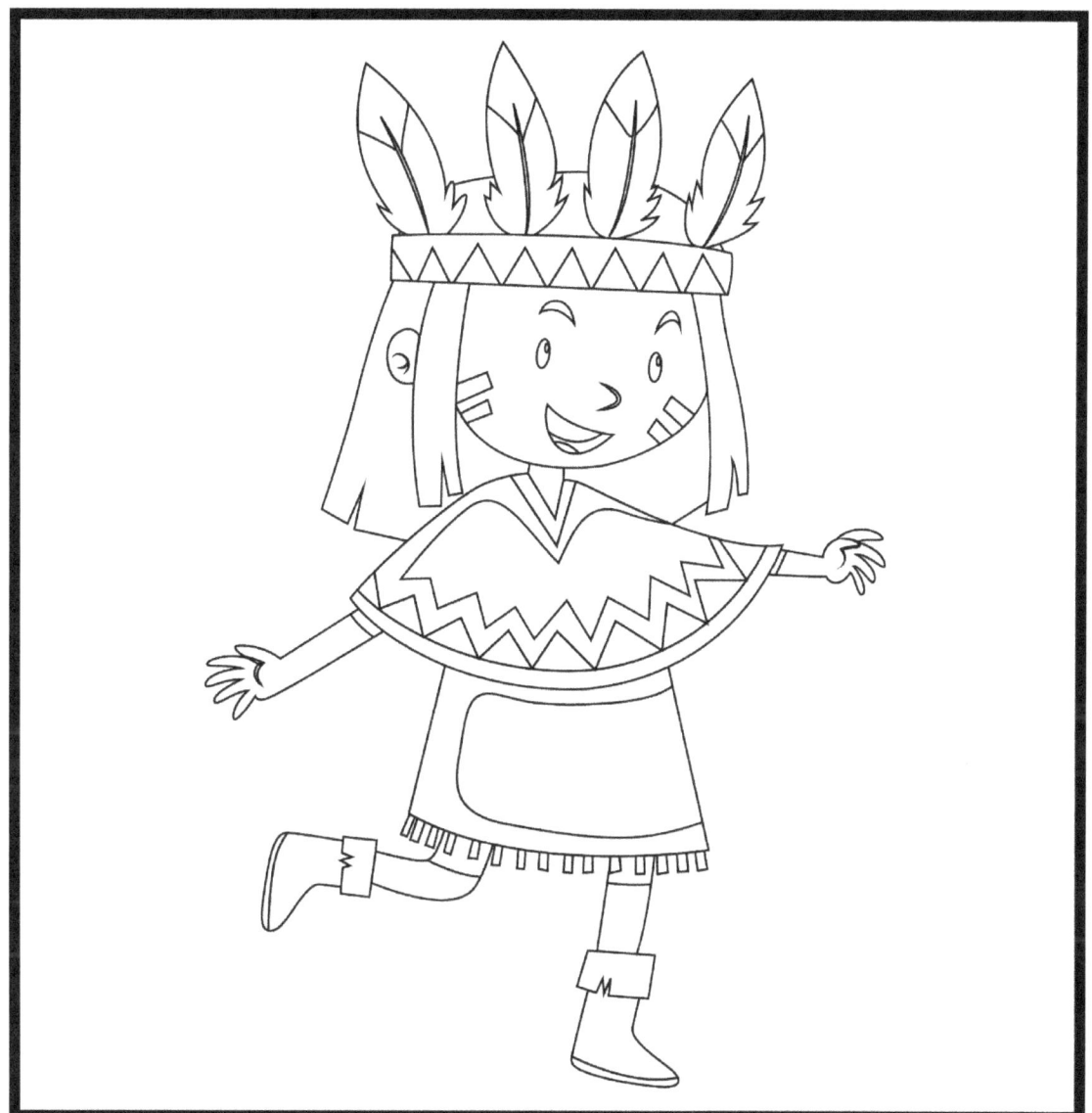

note:

_____

_____

_____

# SEPTEMBER 50TH

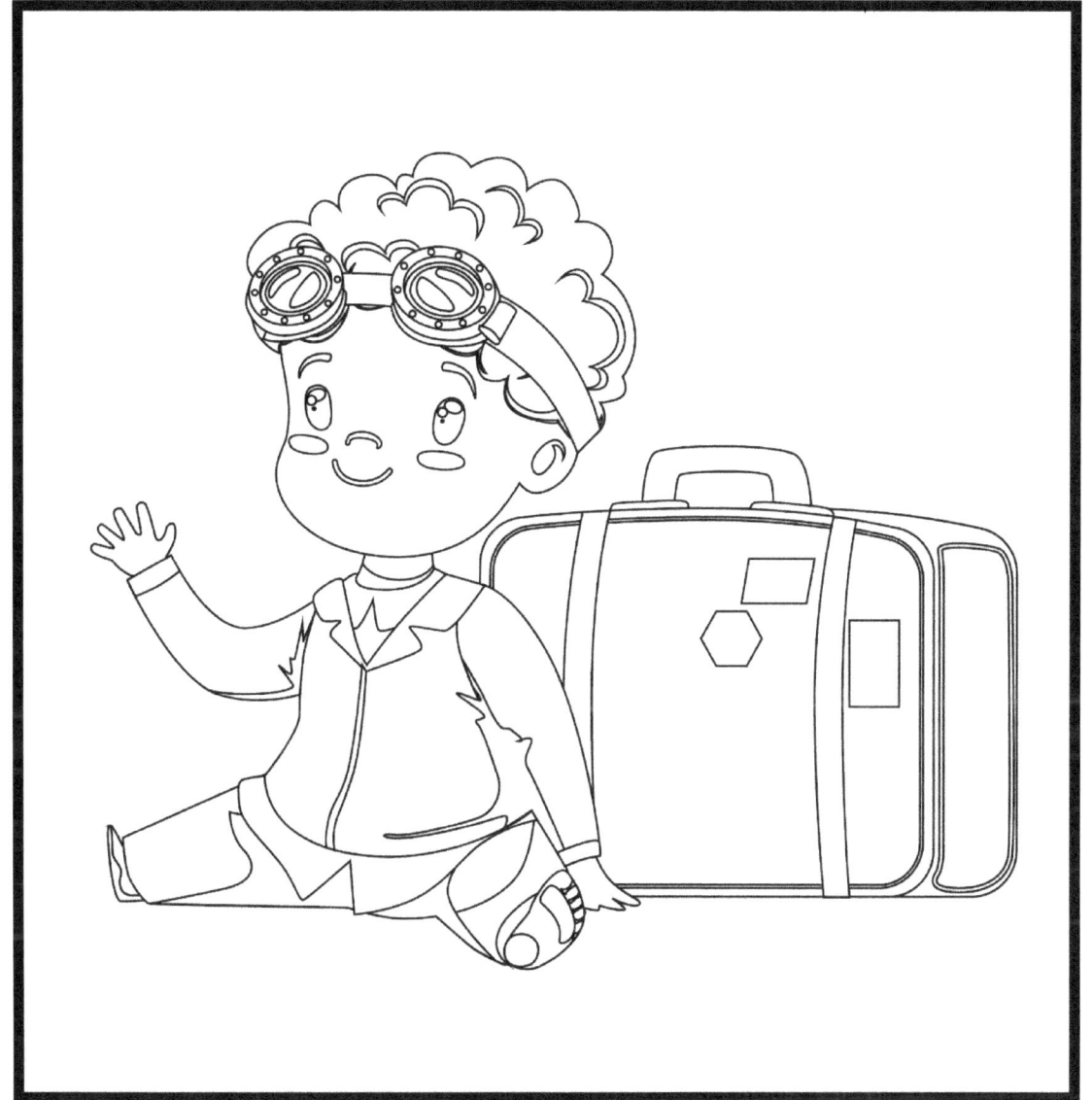

note:

_____

_____

_____

www.ingramcontent.com/pod-product-compliance
Lightning Source LLC
Chambersburg PA
CBHW081607220526
45468CB00010B/2797